Mental Illness

Look for these and other books in the Lucent
Overview series:

Abortion
Acid Rain
Alcoholism
Animal Rights
Artificial Organs
The Beginning of Writing
The Brain
Cancer
Censorship
Child Abuse
Cities
The Collapse of the Soviet Union
Dealing with Death
Death Penalty
Democracy
Drug Abuse
Drugs and Sports
Drug Trafficking
Eating Disorders
Endangered Species
The End of Apartheid in South Africa
Energy Alternatives
Espionage
Euthanasia
Extraterrestrial Life
Family Violence
Gangs
Garbage
Gay Rights
The Greenhouse Effect
Gun Control
Hate Groups
Hazardous Waste
The Holocaust

Homeless Children
Illegal Immigration
Illiteracy
Immigration
Mental Illness
Money
Ocean Pollution
Oil Spills
The Olympic Games
Organ Transplants
Ozone
Pesticides
Police Brutality
Population
Prisons
Rainforests
Recycling
The Reunification of Germany
Schools
Smoking
Space Exploration
Special Effects in the Movies
Teen Alcoholism
Teen Pregnancy
Teen Suicide
The UFO Challenge
The United Nations
The U.S. Congress
The U.S. Presidency
Vanishing Wetlands
Vietnam
World Hunger
Zoos

Mental Illness

by Victoria Sherrow

LUCENT
BOOKS

LUCENT Overview Series

Library of Congress Cataloging-in-Publication Data

Sherrow, Victoria.
    Mental illness / by Victoria Sherrow.
       p. cm. — (Overview series)
    Includes bibliographical references and index.
    ISBN 1-56006-168-5 (lib. bdg. : alk. paper)
    1. Mental illness—Juvenile literature.   [1. Mental illness.]
I. Title.   II. Series: Lucent overview series.
RC460.2.S53   1996
362.2—dc20   95-12284
                                               CIP

Contents

Introduction

WHEN PEOPLE THINK of illness, a physical problem most often comes to mind—pneumonia, diabetes, cancer, or heart disease, for example. Yet the most common diseases in society are mental illnesses, those that affect people's minds and behavior. In his book *Mental Health, Mental Illness*, author Lealon E. Martin writes:

> Mental illness strikes more frequently, attacks more people, requires more prolonged treatment, causes more suffering by the individual and by his family and friends, wastes more human resources, takes up more buildings and other facilities, and consumes more of the personal finances of the individual and his family and the public taxes than any other disease.

Statistics show this to be the case not only in the United States but also in most other industrialized and developing countries.

Millions of people have experienced mental or emotional illnesses themselves or at close range. Mental illness has been defined as a disorder, disease, or disturbance of the mind that prevents a person from functioning adequately in daily life. Mental processes, feelings, and behavior become so impaired as to cause distress to the person and those around him or her. Often this is a matter of degree. Just about everyone feels anxious or depressed sometimes, but ongoing, incapacitating

(Opposite page) Mental disorders affect people's minds and behavior, often impairing their judgment and leaving them anxious or depressed. Millions of people are haunted by mental illnesses, making them the most common diseases in society.

7

anxiety or depression can signal mental illness. Perhaps a family member suffers from a long-term, deep depression or addiction to drugs or alcohol; a relative with Alzheimer's disease cannot recall once-familiar names and faces or remember how to dress; an aunt or cousin is said to have had a "nervous breakdown." Perhaps a friend struggles with incapacitating fears or hears voices nobody else can hear.

Today even someone with no personal experience with mental illness is frequently made aware of it through the media. A popular rock star commits suicide; a film star begins treatment for substance abuse; a politician discloses past psychiatric care for depression; a TV show features homeless mentally ill people; a confessed killer employs an insanity defense.

Startling numbers

Mental diseases affect people of all ages, ethnic groups, and socioeconomic levels. According to a 1993 study conducted by the National Institute of Mental Health (NIMH), about fifty-two million adults, more than one in four, suffer from a mental disorder at some time during a given year. One person in five will have a mental disorder during his or her lifetime.

The personal and social costs of mental illness are reflected in startling numbers. Between 25 and 50 percent of American hospital beds are occupied by mentally ill patients. Suicide is the tenth leading cause of death in the United States, with more than twenty-five thousand suicides occurring each year. Possibly half of the millions of other illness and surgery cases have a mental illness component, and an estimated 75 percent of accidents are also thought to be caused in part by mental illness. Estimates of the annual cost of mental illness in America reach $60 billion.

A psychologist works in a therapeutic garden with several young patients. An estimated 5 to 15 percent of children between the ages of three and fifteen experience chronic mental disorders.

Studies of mental disorders among American children show that some 5 to 15 percent between ages three and fifteen suffer from persistent mental problems. About two million others have severe learning disabilities that put their mental health at risk.

Of the millions of Americans who experience a serious case of depression, many are young people: About 500,000 American teenagers try to kill themselves annually. One of them was Melissa Growth, who attempted suicide in 1992 at age fifteen. An A student and a perfectionist in general, Melissa had felt increasingly anxious and unable to cope with the demands of school and other activities. She took caffeine pills and drank coffee to stay awake late studying, sleeping only about four hours a night. Luckily, on the day Melissa shot herself in the head, her parents found her in time to save her life. She emerged from a deep coma, recovered from her injuries, then began psychological counseling. Once Melissa learned that she did not have to be perfect to be loved, she decided to share her experience publicly to help others, especially teenagers, avoid the same mistake.

One in every four American families will have a member who is mentally ill. These families may suffer greatly. One New York City couple in their sixties has a grown son with schizophrenia, a severe mental illness characterized by disordered thinking patterns, delusions, and paranoia or unrealistic fears. Between 1981 and 1994, he was hospitalized thirty-eight times. Periodically, he stops taking his prescribed antipsychotic medication. As he loses touch with reality and abandons his daily routine, he hears voices and may attack people he thinks plan to hurt him. His parents fear that without ongoing treatment in a supervised housing program, their son may become homeless. "He is not an animal," says his mother. "He happens to be a very intelligent, sensitive person. All he needs is a program or place where he can have some therapy and where he will not be abandoned even if there is something in his psyche that makes him stop his medication."

Children of mentally ill parents face special risks. During an acute episode of her illness, a twenty-nine-year-old mother in Cleveland, Ohio, heard voices that seemed real to her. Social workers, fearing she might be a danger to her young daughter, were forced to remove the child to a foster home. Mental illness of a parent is the third most common reason, after drug abuse and domestic violence, that children are removed from their homes.

Understanding mental illness

Mental disorders come in many forms and range from temporary to chronic. They vary from minor distress or discomfort to major disorders, such as unresponsive depression, or hallucinations, in which people hear or see things that nobody else can hear or see. A person may experience mental illness once, a few times, or on a regular basis. Though people have puzzled over and promoted a number of theories explaining the causes of mental illnesses since ancient times, modern scientists categorize mental conditions as either organic, stemming from a physical cause, or nonorganic, resulting from life experiences.

In the first category, disease, heredity, or injury can result in damage to the brain or nervous system. When the brain is malformed before birth,

A mother provides massage and pool therapy for her twenty-year-old son, who suffered a spinal cord injury. Mental conditions attributed to physical causes such as spinal injuries are categorized as organic.

damaged by disease, or injured physically, symptoms of mental illnesses may result. Brain tumors; hardening of the arteries that carry blood to the brain; destruction of nerve cells as a result of AIDS, syphilis, or Alzheimer's disease; and brain injury from an automobile accident are all organic causes.

But for many mental conditions, no organic cause has yet been identified. To explain these, some doctors and researchers point to the role of a person's environment and life experiences. They say that traumatic life experiences, such as chronic fear, terrible parenting, or persistent abuse can adversely affect a person's psychological and social development and lead to mental illnesses.

Types of mental illnesses

Each person is an individual, with a unique personal and social history. Likewise, no two mentally ill persons have the same type, degree, or progression of symptoms. Nonetheless, some systems of naming various mental illnesses have been developed to provide guidelines for diagnosis and treatment and to enable people around the world to analyze mental illness statistically.

In their most serious forms, mental illnesses are called psychoses. Psychotic conditions involve severe symptoms—delusions, hallucinations, disturbed thinking processes, and an inability to make sound judgments. People may have little or no insight into their behavior, unaware that their impressions do not match outside reality. These severe conditions are usually what people mean when they use the words "insane" or "insanity" to describe someone's behavior.

Mood disorders may be the most widespread types of mental illness. About 20 percent of all Americans will experience a mood disorder at some point in their lives. These disorders include depression, in which a person may experience deep despair, or mania, a state of extreme excitement and elation, marked by racing thoughts and emotions. With a third disorder, manic-depressive illness, people experience episodes of both depression and mania. People suffering from mood disorders often have disturbances in sleep, activity levels, concentration, and interactions with other people. Various forms of depression strike about eighteen million Americans each year.

A forty-year-old nurse and mother of two who went through a severe depression that lasted nearly a year describes the experience:

> I had no desire to get up in the morning, no energy. My arms, legs, all parts of my body felt heavy, like lead. Until this happened, I had always seen myself as a happy, energetic person. Now I was constantly thinking about dying, how I just wanted to die and not feel this way anymore. People around me didn't understand. They would say, "You need to get out more, try some new activities, snap out of it." But I couldn't snap out of it, no matter how hard I tried.

Mental disorders called phobias, characterized by intense fears, are also common. According to the National Institute of Mental Health, some twenty million Americans have at least one phobia severe enough to interfere with their daily life. One that has received publicity in recent years is agoraphobia, an overwhelming sense of panic on leaving one's home.

About two million Americans are affected by schizophrenia, an illness characterized by thought disorders that can lead to unusual, even dangerous, behavior. People with schizophrenia may suffer from delusions in which they think they are a government leader or historical figure, or they may believe certain people intend to harm them. Other symptoms include hallucinations, a flat affect, or lack of visible emotion, a state of extreme detachment from other people, or extremely agitated behavior. Schizophrenia may affect 1 percent of the population at any one time, a sizable number in the United States, where the population reached more than 260 million in the 1990s.

One person with schizophrenia, quoted in a publication from the National Alliance for the Mentally Ill, describes episodes of the illness this way: "It feels like a dream, but it's not, because you're not asleep. And because you're not asleep, you can't wake up." Another says, "My emotions inwardly were at a fever's pitch and it seemed to me that I was only feeling, not thinking."

Another one million Americans suffer from organic psychoses or related conditions caused by diseases of the brain and nervous system. Examples are Alzheimer's disease and senile dementia, the mental illness that occurs in some people as part of aging. Both of these illnesses may cause problems with memory and thinking.

The National Institute of Mental Health also considers substance abuse a category of mental illness. About fourteen million Americans were addicted to alcohol in 1992, while others abused legal or illegal drugs. Alcoholism, drug abuse or addiction, suicidal behavior, and certain other conditions are sometimes called personality disorders.

About 2 to 4 percent of Americans have had a severe anxiety disorder, and still more suffer from a neurosis. Their major symptom is anxiety. Neuroses are sometimes called emotional problems rather than mental illnesses.

Mental illness has been called the most puzzling of all the human phenomena scientists have sought to investigate. It also frequently carries with it a social stigma. For these reasons, the idea

Alzheimer's disease and senile dementia are organic psychoses that often occur as a part of aging. Many elderly people who suffer from these disorders experience problems with their memory and cognitive skills.

of being "crazy" or "out of one's mind" is more frightening to people than is a physical illness or disability.

Throughout history, people have struggled to understand and deal with the personal and social consequences of mental illness. A look at past centuries shows regular shifts in attitudes, as societies variously rebuked, ignored, or offered help to the mentally ill. Societies have struggled to balance the needs and rights of the mentally ill with the needs and rights of the rest of society. Treatments have also changed as new ideas and research gradually replaced more primitive beliefs.

The mentally ill and their families struggle with a variety of personal and social problems. One is the stigma attached to mental illnesses, the idea that they arc not as "real" or legitimate as physical illnesses. Some people believe that those with mental problems are just lazy or lack the willpower to get well. Some mentally ill people are ashamed to seek treatment because they fear being labeled or ostracized. Frequently, those who want help lack access to it for financial reasons or because there are no qualified professionals where they live. These difficulties are compounded by negative attitudes about mental illness and confusion over what to do about it.

Much progress has been made, but problems remain. The search continues for the causes of and cures for many poorly understood mental illnesses. Controversial issues revolve around how society should deal with the mentally ill; for example, what are the legal rights of the mentally ill? And what policies best help the chronically mentally ill, those who are homeless, and those who refuse treatment? Society has debated these dilemmas since ancient times.

Counseling is available for mentally ill individuals. However, many people are too ashamed to seek treatment because they fear they will be ostracized by society.

1

The Long Road to Understanding

Mental illnesses have confused and troubled humankind for thousands of years. Ancient historical records show them to be a persistent feature of the human condition. References to mental disorders can be found in the ancient writings of people in the Middle East, Greece, Rome, India, and China.

Ancient civilizations developed labels for people whose behavior was viewed as extremely unusual, making no sense in terms of external reality. A New Testament reference to mental illness in the Gospel of Luke says that "unclean spirits" came out of a man called "Legion" and were placed in swine, who then died. Legion is called a "demoniac," and the word "demons" has come to stand for madness or emotional struggles. The Egyptians said that a mentally ill person was "not in his right mind" or "smitten with madness." Greeks used phrases such as "lost his wits" and "going out of one's senses" to denote insanity. The Hindus spoke of "stuporous conditions" in which the soul becomes alienated from the body.

Such societies dealt with the mentally ill in various ways, depending on their cultural attitudes and sense of social responsibility. Some viewed

(Opposite page) Throughout history humanity has been confounded by the nature of mental illnesses. In many societies, asylum inmates (pictured) and mentally ill individuals were both ridiculed and feared.

17

The Greek philosopher Plato believed that mentally ill people should be confined to their homes and should only be committed to asylums if they broke the law or threatened public safety.

the mentally ill with fear, hostility, and mistrust or treated them with disgust. Shame attached to mental illness, while physical illness would be viewed with compassion. A few cultures viewed the mentally ill as gifted with special powers and a favored access to the supernatural world.

In ancient times, mentally ill people were not placed in asylums—that is, separate institutions to house them. Communities treated mental illness as a private matter, unless a person broke the law or threatened public safety. In his famous *Laws* (XI), the Greek philosopher Plato states, "If a man is mad, he shall not be at large in the city, but his relations shall keep him at home in any way which they can; or if not, let them pay a penalty." The ancient Romans shared this view.

Wealthy families could care for insane members at home, restraining them if necessary. But the poor or those without relatives roamed the streets. There, they were sometimes ridiculed. People, especially children, might follow them, laughing and throwing stones. Unruly mentally ill people were jailed.

Ancient treatments

Because the ancients lacked scientific knowledge, they often attributed unexplainable conditions to evil spirits. Mentally ill people often sought help from the gods through prayer and by visiting religious shrines. Some wore charms, or amulets, meant to drive away bad spirits. Healers cast special spells; priests tried to draw away, or exorcise, demons thought to cause mental illness.

Some more progressive ways of treating mentally ill people developed in Egypt. One temple medical school near present-day Cairo included a hospital for the mentally ill where they could take part in recreation and pursue useful activities, such as cloth making. Doctors there talked with patients about their problems.

As science developed, people analyzed the causes of illnesses and sought better ways to treat them. Around 400 B.C., the Greek physician Hippocrates listed and described a number of mental and physical illnesses. He declared that mental diseases were as worthy of study and compassion as physical ones and that they had natural causes that could be discovered, such as damaged brain tissues.

Roman physicians also discussed ways in which a person's environment and habits could aggravate mental problems, declaring that grief, excessive anger, lack of rest, worry, and the straining of the senses in work or study could harm one's mental health.

A few physicians advocated compassionate care. Asclepiades of Bithynia, who came to Rome around 91 B.C., refused to isolate mentally ill people in dark rooms. He substituted bright, airy rooms and encouraged patients to exercise and do crafts. Asclepiades recommended music and wine to relax people. In the fourth century A.D., Caelius Aurelianus of Rome, perhaps the greatest physician of his time, promoted the use of therapeutic baths, known as hydrotherapy, and criticized beating and tying up the mentally ill.

For centuries, mental illness was viewed more as a private matter than as a social problem. Families and communities cared for their own. Yet society at large feared and stigmatized the mentally ill. Public attitudes moved gradually from avoidance to hostility to outright persecution, which peaked during the Middle Ages.

Years of persecution

Scientific progress in Europe dwindled during the Middle Ages, from about A.D. 500 to 1500. During these centuries of superstition and fanaticism, mentally ill people were often treated cruelly. No longer a subject of medical study, mental illness entered the realm of magic and witchcraft and was referred to as "devil sickness" or "witch disease." The mentally ill were called "lunaticks" or "fiend-sick." Medieval historians describe public abuse, as when people were sometimes forced to recite sentences like these: "Bind me with chains and fetters as a lunatic who has lost his wits, and keep me in close custody until I repent and recover my senses."

Some mentally ill people suffered during the Inquisition, set up in 1231 by the Catholic Church, the dominant political force in Europe. Inquisition officials arrested and tried people accused of heresy—speaking or acting against

Catholic doctrine. Convicted heretics faced fines, loss of property, beatings, imprisonment, or death. Among those accused of heresy were mentally ill people whose odd behavior led others to charge them with witchcraft and devil worship. Witch-hunts also took place outside the Inquisition, and again, mentally ill people were often victims. By the 1500s, thousands of convicted "witches" had been burned at the stake.

A few brave individuals condemned the Inquisition, saying the so-called witches were mentally ill people who needed help. Yet witch trials continued into the 1600s, both in Europe and in the Massachusetts colony founded in North America.

During the Inquisition, frightened families abandoned mentally ill relatives to wander as outcasts through the towns and countryside, haggard

A medieval woodcut portrays the hanging of a woman declared by the Inquisition to be possessed by demons. Many of those charged with being possessed or with practicing witchcraft were probably suffering from some form of mental illness.

and sickly, often living among animals. Their strange appearance intensified the public's fears. When they went to a new town, they were often whipped, then sent back to their hometowns.

The rise of institutions

In the early Middle Ages, there were few mental institutions in Europe. But with rising numbers of mentally ill people on the streets, towns found ways to isolate them from others. Some were imprisoned; others were placed in general hospitals that housed a few mentally ill patients in their "mad huts" or "mad cells." A few places provided care, but most simply warehoused people who posed problems to society.

There were also a few mental hospitals, mostly dark, dirty places. Some hospitals starved patients or subjected them to icy baths and other harsh "treatments." At London's Bethlehem Royal Hospital, also known as Bedlam, the insane were dressed in rags and ill fed. This facility lacked heat and had poor lighting and ventilation.

A woman is charged with witchcraft during the Salem witch trials in the Massachusetts colony.

Still, most mentally ill people ended up in prison, where they were locked in small cells. Attendants handed them food or necessities through narrow openings. Violent people were attached to the wall with iron collars and metal hoops around their waists. Some towns also got rid of mentally ill people by simply loading them on so-called ships of fools, vessels that moved about the seas, docking at foreign ports.

Mentally ill patients were dressed in rags and subjected to appalling living conditions at Bethlehem Royal Hospital in London.

Studying the mind

The Middle Ages gave way to the Renaissance in the 1500s, with a renewed interest in scientific inquiry and a rejection of superstition. Scientists studied human anatomy, including the brain and nervous tissues. Some prominent physicians and philosophers concluded that mental processes were natural, not supernatural, and could be studied scientifically.

A fanciful painting depicts a doctor performing heat therapy (foreground), a treatment believed to cure patients' fantasies and delusions. During the Renaissance, physicians rejected superstition in favor of scientific inquiry.

Some scientists speculated about the causes of mental illnesses, pointing to a brain that was "too dry" or "bad elements" that got inside the blood. Some thought a disease in a particular organ, such as the spleen, caused a corresponding mental disease, such as extreme depression.

The call for moral treatment

Although scientists were trying to learn more about mental illness during the 1700s, little could be done to treat it. Social attitudes toward the afflicted did not improve much, and mistreatment was common. During the economic depression of the 1600s and 1700s, indigent people, including many mentally ill, were imprisoned and used as a source of free forced labor.

With the onset of the Industrial Revolution, people moved from farms and villages to take factory jobs in cities. In densely populated, poorly serviced cities, more mentally ill people were abandoned and left to roam the streets, where they often upset others. Communities sought to confine them, along with physically handicapped people, the very poor, and criminals, all of whom were considered outcasts.

By the late 1700s, a few mental hospitals were humane, but most were not. They kept the mentally ill away from the public but did not help them. Many patients were beaten and subjected to bloodletting and purgatives, substances that caused vomiting. Their heads were shaved and blistered to let out bad vapors that might be trapped in the brain. In 1785, the inspector general of French hospitals and prisons reported:

> Thousands of lunatics are locked up in prisons without anyone even thinking of administering the slightest remedy. The half-mad are mingled with those who are totally deranged, those who rage with those who are quiet; some are in chains while others are free in their prison.

Reformers in several countries called for more humane treatment. In England, William Tuke, a tea and coffee merchant, protested the chaining of mental patients. A devout Quaker, Tuke believed in aiding the less fortunate. He established the

The York Retreat for the Mentally Ill was established in 1796 by Quaker William Tuke. The English hospital provided compassionate treatment for mentally ill patients in an orderly atmosphere.

York Retreat for the Mentally Ill in 1796, where patients received kind treatment in a clean, orderly atmosphere. Vincenzo Chiarugi led a reform movement in Italy, establishing a humane hospital in 1788 in Florence.

In France, Dr. Philippe Pinel launched a pioneering effort to help the mentally ill. Pinel, a founder of modern psychiatry, specialized in observing mental patients and classifying their conditions. He thought that medical practice should be based on research and facts and rejected bleeding, physical punishment, and other treatments that seemed ineffective. During the 1790s, Pinel became the chief physician at Bicêtre and Salpêtrière, both Parisian asylums where people were bound, and ordered the inmates to be unchained. He said, "To detain maniacs in constant seclusion, and to load them with chains; to leave them defenceless, to the brutality of underlings . . . is a system of superintendence more distinguished for its convenience than for its humanity or its success."

French physician Philippe Pinel demands the removal of chains from the mentally ill at the Bicêtre asylum in Paris. A pioneer in the field of psychiatry, Pinel declared that scientific research and moral treatment should be the basis for medical practice.

Dr. Philippe Pinel helped to reform abusive asylums like Salpêtrière (pictured) in Paris. Rather than leaving inmates in seclusion or bound in chains, Pinel asserted that mentally ill patients should receive moral treatment aimed at recovery.

In 1794, Pinel wrote that treatment of the mentally ill "should reflect a well-ordered wisdom corresponding to the varied needs of the insane and proclaim from afar the respect due to distress and misfortune." He proposed a system called moral treatment, in which patients would stay in well-organized asylums where they would learn to use their reasoning abilities and have hope of recovering.

In America, moral treatment was supported by religious New Englanders, including Puritans, Quakers, and Unitarians, whose beliefs included a duty to serve others. Pennsylvania Hospital, founded in 1756 by Benjamin Franklin and Philadelphia Quakers, included a wing for the mentally ill.

The first public hospital solely for the mentally ill in British North America was built in the Virginia colony. In 1766, Governor Francis Fauquier had given an address describing the mentally ill as "a poor unhappy set of People who are deprived of their senses and wander about the Country terrifying the Rest of their Fellow Creatures." Fauquier suggested the colony build a mental hospital where physicians could "endeavor to restore to them their lost Reason." The Public Hospital for Persons of Insane or Disordered Minds was opened in Williamsburg, Virginia, in 1773.

Treatment of the mentally ill here and at other hospitals of that era reflected public fear and frustration and the lack of effective medications or cures. Most illnesses were treated alike. Among the various treatments were such long-standing ones as water therapy, herbs, bleeding, restraints, enemas, and purgatives. Dunking chairs were used to calm violent people or arouse indifferent ones by plunging them into hot or cold water. An electrostatic generator machine for delivering shocks became available around 1793. In the early 1800s, a type of waistcoat, later called a straitjacket, came into use as a better restraint than chains and waist hoops. Patients were also

The Public Hospital for Persons of Insane or Disordered Minds was founded in Williamsburg, Virginia, in 1773. Like many other institutions of this era, the hospital's treatment of the mentally ill was based on public fear and a lack of effective medications.

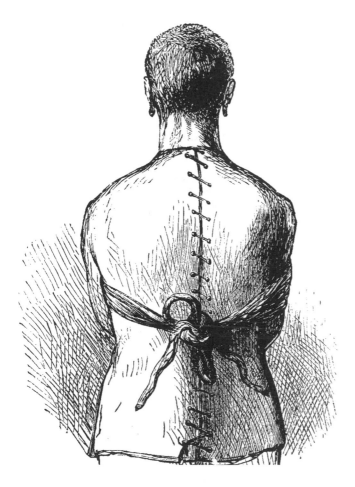

bound to a chair with leather or iron straps. These methods might seem uncaring, but many doctors thought they might help mentally ill patients. Some doctors also believed strong measures might lead people to choose sanity over insanity.

During the late 1700s, Philadelphia physician Benjamin Rush, called the founder of American psychiatry, suggested that patients fared better when they were housed in clean spaces, treated gently, and encouraged to exercise and keep busy. Yet even Dr. Rush felt compelled to restrain some patients and to use the common practices of bloodletting and "ducking" agitated patients into cold water.

By the early 1800s, American physicians, scholars, scientists, and informed citizens were discussing hospital-based care for the mentally ill. Donations from wealthy citizens helped to build mental asylums in Boston; New York City; Philadelphia; Hartford, Connecticut; and many other places. Some were modeled after the benevolent York Retreat in England.

Most institutionalized patients were severely ill, and many were brought by families who could no longer cope with their behavior. While visiting a New York asylum in 1817, Dr. William Handy observed a young adult male who was "gloomy, sullen, discontented" with periods of "maniacal symptoms." A middle-aged female patient had told her family that she must kill one of them, then be imprisoned and executed. She was also convinced that "the devil reigned."

As time passed, many asylums, with no other means of support, became private hospitals, admitting only patients who could pay for care. Reformers were dismayed to find many poor mentally ill people in prisons. Reverend Louis Dwight discovered inmates who had not left their cells for eight or nine years. Dwight described one wretched man clothed in "a wreath of rags" in a cell with "no bed, chair or bench . . . light, heat, or air."

To house these people, states built more public mental hospitals during the early 1800s. This effort coincided with the growth of other state-operated institutions, such as schools, juvenile homes, and prisons, and signaled a transition to state responsibility for matters that had once been handled by families and local communities.

Troubled asylums

The moral treatment movement that began during the 1700s recommended that patients be involved in work and occupational therapy, recreation, religion, education, and group life. However, in most settings this movement was short-lived.

In most state-run hospitals, treatment was limited. Their major role was custodial, and they protected people from harming themselves or others. Overcrowding was common, especially as immigration brought more people to America during the late 1800s. Between 1875 and 1924, immigration laws banned people with physical or mental disorders from entering the United States. But there was no sure way to tell who was mentally ill or to predict an immigrant's future mental health. Since immigrants were usually poor, those with mental illnesses often ended up in public asylums.

Institutional life could be grim. Frustrated by patients' rash behavior, staffs at asylums often used mechanical restraints. Inmates were kept in straitjackets and fastened into tranquilizer chairs, some of which whirled at speeds of one hundred revolutions per minute. Many patients were shackled, some for years at a time.

Forced commitments

Many patients who were eventually released claimed they had been abused, used for free labor, or sexually assaulted in custody. Author Phyllis Chesler studied the histories of nineteenth-century women who were in asylums. Many reported being forced to do the dirtiest chores, such as cleaning up fellow patients' excrement. Those who refused were punished. A woman named Priscilla said that attendants "ganged up on me. They put a sheet over me, threw me down to the floor, and began punching and kicking me."

At the time, people could be committed, confined in asylums, and treated against their will. Some were not truly insane, but a family member

Many asylums resorted to the use of mechanical restraints like this tranquilizer chair. Mentally ill patients would be fastened into the chair and bound with leather or iron straps.

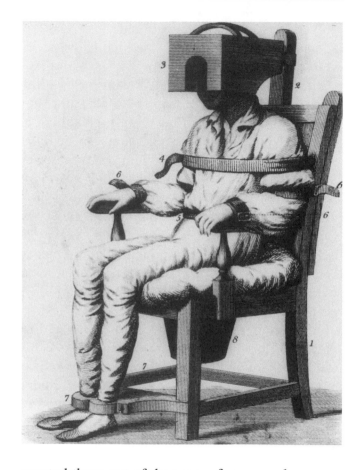

wanted them out of the way—for example, someone who wanted to get rid of a spouse. At that time, commitment laws were broad, allowing people to be committed fairly easily. Some patients were forcibly given shock treatments, in which electrical shocks were applied to their heads. Many had no medical care. Elizabeth P. Ware Packard was committed to an asylum during the mid-1800s and later released. In her book *Modern Persecution* she wrote:

> Many patients were received and discharged, while I was there, who never had five minutes' conversation with the Doctors while in the Asylum. Often the new arrival would . . . inquire, "When am I to have an examination?" I would reply, "You never have an examination after you get

here, for the Doctor receives you on the representation of those who want you should stay here."

Some paupers were sent to city or county mental hospitals, such as New York's Blackwell's Island and the Boston Lunatic Asylum. State institutions teemed with chronically mentally ill people. They were often dirty and lacked suitable accommodations, adequate food, and capable staff members. Often, political connections, not training, determined who was given jobs in these government institutions.

Reformers gain public attention

Reformers began to expose poorly run asylums. In 1887, a newspaper reporter named Nellie

The county mental hospital at Blackwell's Island in New York often had too many patients. Like most state institutions, Blackwell's lacked suitable accommodations and competent staff.

Bly faked insanity so that she could write an undercover story about conditions at Blackwell's Island. After being committed, Bly spent ten days at the asylum, where all her belongings were taken from her and she was made to wear a patched dress. Her article "Behind Asylum Bars" shocked readers of the the *New York World* newspaper. Bly described inedible food, cramped conditions, and brutal attendants who beat patients and doused them with cold water. She also said that some inmates were not insane.

A public outcry resulted from Bly's articles, and a grand jury investigated Blackwell's Island. More than $200,000 was allocated to improve rooms and food and to hire more qualified physicians. Public concern increased as reformers continued to point out the awful conditions in mental hospitals. People decried cases in which patients were unjustly committed or shackled for years at a time. New state laws set standards that hospitals must meet in order to operate legally, and a system of regular inspection was established.

The best-known American reformer was Dorothea Lynde Dix, a schoolteacher from Maine. In 1841, while teaching a religious class for jail inmates in East Cambridge, Massachusetts, Dix was appalled to see mentally ill people confined with criminals and mistreated. For eighteen months, she studied mental institutions in Massachusetts.

Dix's written report was presented to the state legislature in 1843. She told legislators, "I come as the advocate of helpless, forgotten, insane, idiotic men and women; of beings sunk to conditions from which the most unconcerned would start with real horror." Dix and her supporters inspired the state to reform its institutions. She devoted the rest of her life to helping the mentally ill in New England, then in other parts of the

Dorothea Lynde Dix was instrumental in the reformation of mental institutions in Massachusetts during the 1840s. Dix's efforts inspired hospital reform throughout the United States, Canada, and Europe.

country, and Canada. Her efforts sparked the creation or enlargement of more than thirty mental hospitals in the United States, and roused Europeans to improve conditions for the mentally ill there, as well.

Government and institutions respond

As the reform movement spread, state governments appointed committees to study mental institutions. Members of the Virginia legislature inspected the Public Hospital in Williamsburg in 1835 and issued a critical report. Typically, the report stated, patients were awakened at dawn when their cells were unlocked. After they were cleaned, patients were taken to sitting rooms or left in their cells. A few women sewed during the day, but most patients were idle. Patients ate meals apart from the staff and from each other and were not permitted knives or forks. At night they slept on straw mattresses inside locked cells.

When members of the Virginia legislature inspected the Public Hospital in Williamsburg they were revolted by the conditions. Most patients were idle during the day and at night they slept on straw mattresses inside locked cells.

Under the adminstration of Dr. John Minson Galt II, the Public Hospital in Williamsburg, Virginia, was tranformed into a "benevolent institution." Patients' rooms were improved and the hospital emphasized social contact and rehabilitation.

The committee suggested ways to change the hospital into a "benevolent institution," emphasizing social contact and rehabilitation. Patients were given better clothing and encouraged to work in a large vegetable garden and to learn skills, such as tailoring. They were urged to play games and musical instruments. Some went into town or attended church with staff members. From 1841 to 1862, under administrator Dr. John Minson Galt II, the hospital made the patients' rooms more attractive, held dances, and used minimal restraints. Galt called the insane "our brethren" and said that the gap between sanity and insanity was small. He also insisted that patients improved with respectful treatment.

In 1857, Galt suggested a radical approach to patient care. Galt wanted to deinstitutionalize—remove from the asylum—many patients, removing barriers between mentally ill people and the rest of society. He believed some patients could board with residents of the neighboring community. Other patients could work at jobs in town by day and return to the asylum at night. Still others, Galt said, were capable of living and working at a farm managed by the hospital staff.

Galt's proposals were widely criticized. People still preferred to separate those with mental illnesses from others. Not until the medical breakthroughs of the 1900s did many people consider mentally ill people fit to live in mainstream society.

Meanwhile, the number of institutions continued to grow. By 1880, there were nearly 140 public and private mental hospitals in the United States, holding about 41,000 patients. Nine asylums had patient populations of nearly 1,000, but the average size was around 500.

Institutional treatments of the late nineteenth century were limited to electrical shocks, hypnosis, water therapy, massage, and doses of substances called bromides to calm agitated people. Drugs made from the opium plant had a calming effect but caused undesirable side effects and addiction. More effective treatments were years away.

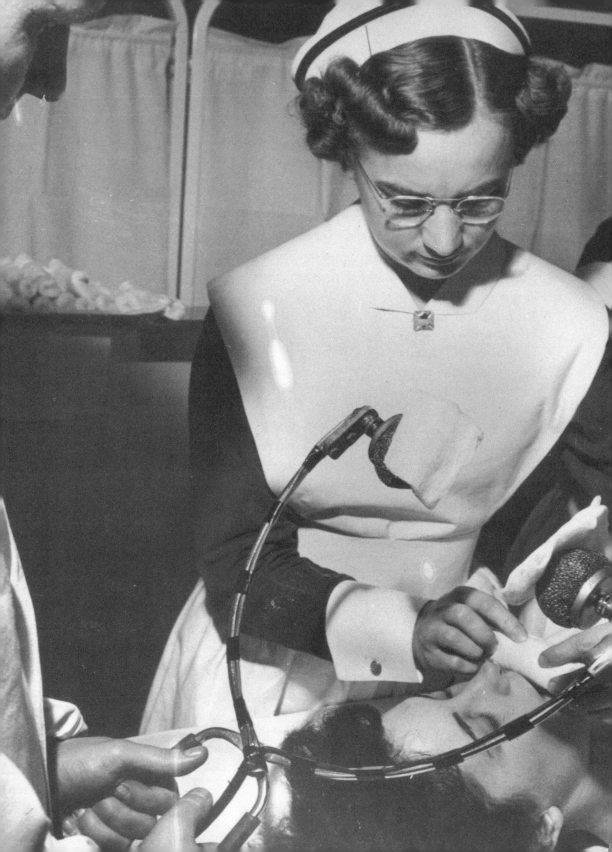

2

Expanding Knowledge and Treatment

THE SOCIAL REFORM efforts of the 1800s resulted in more mental hospitals, a push toward more humane treatment, and some laws to protect the rights of the mentally ill. During these years, researchers intensified their study of mental illnesses and developed new approaches to treatment. Beginning in the late 1800s, effective new physical and psychological therapies emerged, including medications to help the chronically ill and reduce the most severe symptoms of mental illness.

Gaining information about mental illness

As more mental institutions opened, the people who worked with patients sought to learn more about mental illnesses, and then shared their insights. Numerous books, articles, and other materials about mental illness, psychology, and human behavior were published. Written materials and lectures promoted knowledge and discussion about mental illness in the United States.

During the 1800s, the study of mental illnesses became for the first time part of the medical

(Opposite page) The study of mental illness increased following the social reform movement of the 1800s. With this expanding knowledge came new approaches to treating mental illnesses, including the use of electroshock therapy (pictured).

school curriculum. Dr. Benjamin Rush had published *Medical Inquiries and Observations upon the Diseases of the Mind* in 1812, the only psychiatric textbook published in America before 1883. During the 1800s, surgery and psychiatry developed into the two first medical specialties.

Early in the 1800s, organizations to help mental patients were formed. The Association of Medical Superintendents of American Institutions for the Insane (AMSAII) was made up of the directors of mental institutions, almost always physicians. The AMSAII later became the American Psychiatric Association and began publication of the *American Journal of Insanity*. This journal aimed to interest professionals from other fields, such as law and religion, in the prevention and cure of mental illness. Publications like these helped to bring the subject of mental illness more into the open.

Just another disease?

Still seeking the causes of mental illness, many scientists of the time leaned toward biological explanations. In an *American Journal of Insanity* article from the early 1800s, Amariah Brigham, the superintendent of Utica State Hospital in New York, wrote:

> The truth appears to be that the brain is the instrument which the mind uses in this life, to manifest itself and, like all other parts of our bodies, is liable to disease, and when diseased, is often incapable of manifesting harmoniously and perfectly the powers of the mind.

This interpretation disputed the idea that mentally ill people were somehow to blame for their strange behavior. It put mental illness in the same category as other medical conditions. But the mentally ill still faced the negative social attitudes. In the late 1800s, Dr. Thomas S. Kirkbride reminded people that mentally ill people were human and that any human being might suffer such a fate. He wrote, "Insanity should be classed with other diseases. . . . It should never be forgotten that every individual who has a brain is liable to insanity, precisely as everyone with a stomach runs the risk at some period of being a martyr to dyspepsia [digestive problems]."

Searching for clues in the brain

Eager to unravel the mystery of mental illness, scientists of the 1800s focused on learning how the brain works. Some thought it was divided into discrete compartments, each of which regulated memory, conscience, understanding, imagination, passions, religion, or morals. They theorized that specific mental problems resulted from injuries to different compartments of the brain. Other scientists speculated that certain people were born with brains that were highly susceptible to developing mental illness. Such a tendency might be inherited, they said, since mental illness seemed to run in some families.

Benjamin Rush considered how both physical problems and a person's way of life might cause mental illness. He said that insanity could result from problems with blood vessels in the brain or damage to the central nervous system, such as injured tissues. He also looked at the role of mental and emotional stress. Overworking the memory or having a job that required frequent mental transitions from one subject to the other might cause insanity, Rush suggested. He advised people to exercise their minds in order to avoid senility.

Many doctors, frustrated by the lack of effective cures for mental illnesses, aimed instead at preventing some problems altogether. This preventive approach coincided with the early public health movement in America in the late 1800s.

People worried about the impact of urban squalor and overcrowding on people's health called for better sanitation, labor reform, prison reform, and the prohibition of alcohol. Experts recommended a healthy diet, education, exercise, clean air, and healthy habits of thought and emotional expression. Many urged the public to turn to morality and religion.

As part of a movement to prevent mental illness, child rearing became an important subject of research and instruction. Mothers were advised to read about infant care and to attend lectures and discussions about moral upbringing. Books and articles about how to balance the physical, moral, and intellectual growth of children were increasingly popular.

The development of psychotherapy

Meanwhile, scientists worldwide continued to explore other possible causes of mental illness. The work of Sigmund Freud revolutionized the field of psychiatry and transformed popular understanding of mental illness and human development in general. Born near Vienna, Austria, in 1856, Freud was a medical doctor trained as a neurophysiologist, a scientist who studies the structure and functioning of the nervous system. In Paris, he had studied with a French neurologist, Jean-Martin Charcot, who used hypnosis to treat hysterical paralysis, that is, a paralysis brought on by mental, not physical, causes.

During the 1880s, Freud noticed that while under hypnosis some mental hospital patients recalled earlier life experiences that seemed to explain their current problems. In his autobiography, he wrote, "I received the profoundest impression of the possibility that there could be powerful mental processes which nevertheless remained hidden from the consciousness of men." He tried vari-

Sigmund Freud radically changed the field of psychiatry with his theory of psychoanalysis. Freud contended that unresolved conflicts could lead to mental illness.

ous ways of encouraging patients to retrieve long-buried memories, which he claimed were stored at a level of the mind called the unconscious.

From this work, Freud developed the theory of psychoanalysis, which stresses the role of the unconscious in mental illness. He wrote numerous papers based on his studies of patients' dreams and mental processes. Near the turn of the century, Freud theorized that neuroses result from childhood experiences, such as continual rejection by a parent, that prevent people from developing normally. According to Freud, unresolved conflicts could lead to mental illness, with symptoms such as severe anxiety or irrational fears and behaviors.

Freud's approach became the basis of psychologically oriented, as opposed to physical, treatment of mental illness. Psychoanalytic treatment encouraged patients to examine their dreams as the symbols of repressed, or buried, thoughts. Therapists wanted patients to remember events and "free associate"—verbalize any and all thoughts that came to mind—with little comment from the neutral therapist. This kind of therapy, aimed at resolving hidden conflict, became known as a "talking cure."

Freud's ideas were criticized as well as praised. Some physicians called his methods unscientific. Others said that while Freud had explained how mental illness might occur, his form of treatment did not help all patients and took a great deal of time, sometimes years. Nonetheless, the practice of psychoanalysis spread throughout Europe and to North America. Generations of psychiatrists (medical doctors who study and treat mental illnesses) and psychologists (people who study mental processes and human behavior) have built upon or branched away from Freud's work.

New physical treatments

In 1895, Boston surgeon Harvey Cushing performed the first brain surgery in the United States. Cushing had observed brain surgery in London and pioneered a slow, careful method of removing tumors. Eventually, he and other surgeons were able to remove brain tumors without serious complications, making it possible to cure patients whose mental symptoms were caused by tumors that disturbed the functioning of their brains.

Other new physical treatments yielded mixed results. Medical researchers had found that an overdose of insulin, a digestive hormone secreted by the pancreas, caused the body to go into an in-

Boston surgeon Harvey Cushing performed the first brain surgery in the United States in 1895. This revolutionary surgery allowed doctors to remove brain tumors, thereby curing many patients of mental disorders.

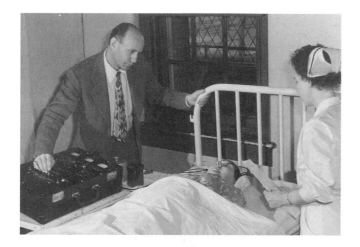

A mental institution patient receives electroshock therapy. Electrodes on the patient's skull allow electrical currents to shock the brain in an attempt to rearrange brain patterns and minimize symptoms.

tense shock, which incidentally had a calming effect. Psychiatrists used insulin and another chemical called metrazol to induce shocks in schizophrenics who displayed frenzied or violent behavior. By 1940, all American mental hospitals had adopted the practice, but despite slightly positive results, inducing insulin shock proved dangerous and even fatal in a few cases and was eventually abandoned.

A new way of producing seizures, electroconvulsive therapy (ECT, or electroshock therapy), was also widely used to treat psychosis. After anesthetizing the patient, doctors placed electrodes on the skull and applied electrical currents. It was thought that these shocks could rearrange disordered brain patterns, reducing symptoms. Some patients reported improvement after electroconvulsive treatments, but others complained of harmful side effects, such as memory loss.

A controversial practice called psychosurgery emerged during the 1930s. Scientists found that removing the frontal lobes of the brains of animals or severing the nerve fibers between the brain's front lobes and the rest of the brain, called a lobotomy, rendered them less aggressive. Operating from that model on the mentally ill, many

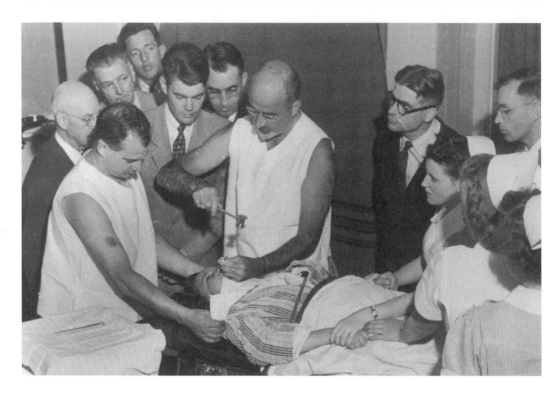

Surgeons perform a lobotomy, a once popular treatment for chronic mental illnesses. Lobotomies tended to curtail violent behavior, but they also left many patients with severe brain damage.

doctors used a technique in which they drilled holes in the skull. They then inserted and rotated a knife in order to destroy the brain cells between a part of the brain called the thalamus and the prefrontal lobes.

This irreversible surgery became a popular treatment for severe mental disorders. By 1960, about fifty thousand lobotomies had been performed in America, most on patients labeled incurable. Lobotomies reduced violent behavior in some patients but did not restore normal functioning. Many were left in a vegetative state, with severe brain damage; others developed seizure disorders. About 5 percent died.

Controversial from the start, the drastic treatments prompted debate in and out of the medical community. Their use posed ethical dilemmas. Many were experimental, and opponents claimed it was wrong to use them on people who were not capable of making rational choices about their treatment. On the other hand, supporters argued that patients who seemed hopelessly ill should have access to anything that might conceivably help them.

Many critics of physical treatments were doctors who preferred nonphysical, psychological approaches. One of them, William Alanson White, wrote to a fellow physician:

> I have a suspicion that some of these schizophrenic patients get well with insulin shock treatment and other similar methods that are exceedingly painful and disagreeable in order to get out of the sanitarium where they use such methods or at least to escape their repetition.

By the 1930s, doctors could visualize blood vessels and parts of the brain with improved X-ray techniques. A German psychiatrist named Hans Berger recorded brain waves with an electroencephalograph, and scientists could for the first time compare the brain-wave patterns of patients with different mental illnesses. It was hoped that new knowledge about the brain would lead to a better understanding of its normal and abnormal functioning.

In 1906, Spanish scientist Santiago Ramón y Cajal won a Nobel Prize for his discovery that neurons are separate cells connected by tissue called synapses, laying the groundwork for research that explained how malfunctions of nerve connections or the chemicals that transmitted nerve messages might cause mental disorders. By understanding these chemical interactions, scientists hoped to discover medications that would alleviate mental symptoms.

The work of Spanish scientist Santiago Ramón y Cajal helped scientists to understand how nerve malfunctions could result in mental disorders.

New drug treatments

Effective medications were the most welcome new physical treatments to emerge during the

1900s. Acute schizophrenia, in particular, and other psychoses had long resisted all treatment methods. In fact, the number of people diagnosed with schizophrenia had risen steadily during the nineteenth and twentieth centuries, although nobody was sure why. In 1904, about two out of every one thousand Americans were diagnosed as schizophrenic. By 1955, that number had doubled. About half of the patients in mental hospitals were diagnosed as schizophrenic, and many were doomed to spend the rest of their lives confined to institutions and suffering from chronic, disabling symptoms.

The effects of chlorpromazine

In 1954, a tranquilizer called chlorpromazine became available for people with schizophrenia and mania, an aspect of manic-depressive disorder. Chlorpromazine calmed people in a more precise manner than did sedatives in use up to that time. Previously, drugs had calmed patients by sedating the entire nervous system, resulting in many side effects and leaving people numbed and lethargic.

With chlorpromazine, those who worked with seriously ill patients in mental institutions reported dramatically different results. Dr. Frank Ayd wrote that in the past, patients in the disturbed ward of the hospital had been "screaming, combative individuals whose animalistic behavior required restraint and seclusion":

> Catatonic patients stood day after day, rigid as statues, their legs swollen and bursting. . . . Their comrades idled week after week, lying on hard benches or the floor, deteriorating, aware only of their delusions and hallucinations. . . . Periodically the air was pierced by the shouts of a raving patient. Suddenly, without notice, like an erupting volcano, a [violently active] schizophrenic bursts into frenetic behavior, lashing out at others or

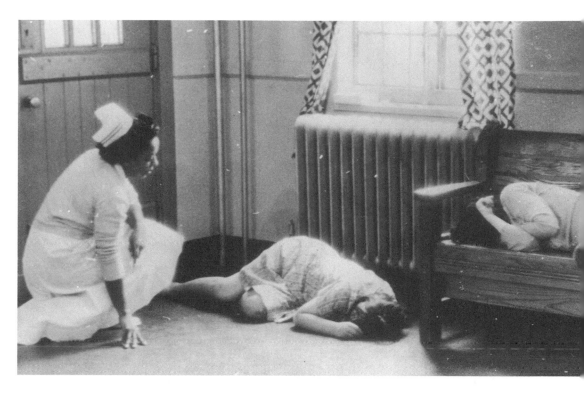

striking himself with his fists, or running wildly and aimlessly about.

Walking through a state mental hospital in New York after chlorpromazine was introduced, Dr. Henry Brill described patients as "dressed, quiet, cooperative, and in surprisingly good contact—with their psychiatric symptoms wiped away."

Other "miracle" drugs appeared in the years that followed, including minor and major tranquilizers to calm overly excited and agitated patients, sedatives to promote sleep, and drugs to alleviate depression. Some were discovered by accident by scientists working on other problems, but soon drug companies decided to look for specific formulas to treat specific mental problems. Some pharmaceutical research was based on evidence that certain illnesses arose because of chemical imbalances in the body. Among the most successful results was lithium, a medication

The introduction of drug therapy had varied effects on mentally ill patients. Some previously combative individuals became calm and cooperative, while others experienced catatonic states and were content to lie motionless on benches or floors.

A psychiatrist studies his patient's reaction to problem pictures during a counseling session. Many psychiatrists believe that analysis of repressed feelings or emotional conflicts is more helpful than treatment using medications.

used to control the manic, or overly excited, phase of manic-depressive disorder. Before long lithium became the standard treatment for manic-depressive illness, reducing the violent mood swings that plagued so many patients and often replacing psychoanalytic treatment.

As more effective new drugs were introduced, people realized that behavior could be changed with medications that altered the faulty biochemistry of the brain. Physicians had new and powerful tools to use in the fight against mental illness.

Changing views of treatment

By the 1950s, several new medications, as well as a growing body of research about human behavior, aided people working with the mentally ill. Psychoanalytic psychiatrists and biological psychiatrists considered various treatment choices and debated which helped patients more—the use of medications or psychotherapy. There were also those who believed in blending different approaches, depending on individual patient needs.

Along with these approaches, another treatment called milieu therapy, or the therapeutic community, became popular. It was based on the idea that the environment at mental institutions could be designed in ways that helped mentally ill persons become well and return to society. One who pioneered this approach was British psychiatrist Maxwell Jones, who set up therapeutic communities for mentally ill servicemen after World War II. Jones said that the hospital community could be "an active force in treatment." Well-planned hospital environments, he believed, could help patients learn more effective ways of handling their problems. They could give patients the message that they were worthy and capable. Faulty milieus could reinforce a patient's dysfunctional behaviors and convey a sense of hopelessness, said supporters of milieu therapy. In 1960, Dr. Robert N. Rapoport wrote:

> The hospital is not seen as a place where patients are classified and stored, nor a place where one group of individuals (the medical staff) gives treatment to another group of individuals (the patients) according to the model of general medical hospitals; but as a place which is organized as a community in which everyone is expected to make some contribution towards the shared goals of creating a social organization that will have healing properties.

Physicians, psychologists, nurses, and social workers were among those who suggested ways to make hospitals more healing environments for patients. In a therapeutic community, patients were encouraged to become more involved in their own treatment. Patients attended meetings

To make hospitals more therapeutic, mentally ill patients were encouraged to become more involved in their own treatment by attending meetings, performing chores, and participating in occupational therapy classes (pictured).

with hospital staff members, performed various chores, and took part in decision making rather than assume the passive role or withdrawal of the past. The view that mentally ill people had much to contribute and should be actively involved in organizing their lives signaled new attitudes in mental health care. Milieu therapy, used mostly in private psychiatric facilities, showed encouraging results.

As the idea of therapeutic communities spread, some hospital staffs took another step and developed "open-door hospitals." Worried that patients might face negative attitudes or discrimination after leaving the hospital, they allowed patients to leave the hospital community for designated periods followed by readmission. They also involved family members in the healing process by holding family therapy sessions along with individual psychotherapy. Group therapy was another way to help patients learn more effective ways of relating to other people.

By 1960, there was a great deal of optimism in the field of mental health. Medications to relieve severe symptoms, various types of psychotherapy for individuals and groups, therapeutic environments in mental hospitals—all these enjoyed wide support.

Mental health professionals began discussing what kinds of services might enable mentally ill people to live in the community, whenever possible. At the same time, other political and social forces combined to create the atmosphere that gave rise to the community mental health movement in America.

3

The Community Mental Health Movement

IN FEBRUARY 1963, President John F. Kennedy made a historic speech before Congress on the subject of mental illness. Kennedy discussed the shortcomings of state mental institutions and called for "a bold new approach" to helping the mentally ill, including the establishment of community mental health centers.

By the 1960s, the stage had been set for such an approach. Attitudes toward mental illness and the most effective and humane ways to help people had changed. New medications had been shown to reduce some severe mental symptoms. Politicians, mental health professionals, and others spoke out on behalf of the mentally ill, challenging the long-standing stigma against them. The government took a more active role in promoting mental health and making services available to more people throughout the country.

Scientists showed a heightened interest in how society itself influences people's behavior. The focus moved toward the ideal of promoting mental health and preventing illness, when possible. All this fostered a crusade to move people

(Opposite page) Three brothers relax on the steps of their new community-based home after being released from a mental institution. Changing attitudes toward mental illness led many individuals to urge the return of mental patients to the community.

55

out of mental institutions and back into the community.

Military influences

After World War II, the federal government assumed a much more active role in formulating mental health policy than ever before. During the war, the government had come to realize the scope of mental illness in America. About 4.8 million draftees (or 18 percent) were rejected for reasons of mental illness. One million—43 percent—of the disability discharges from the armed services during the war were given for neuropsychiatric reasons.

Military psychiatrists had initially helped to screen individuals who seemed mentally unfit for

The community mental health movement made services available to people across the country. This psychiatrist counsels a disturbed man at an outpatient clinic.

service. As the war went on, their role increased greatly. Large numbers of military personnel developed mental disorders under the prolonged stress and adversities of wartime service. Experts in the Army Medical Corps concluded that these stresses were so great that just about anyone was susceptible to a mental breakdown under the circumstances. They sought ways to reduce stress on servicepeople through preventive measures, such as limiting the time soldiers spent in combat zones and allowing for regular rest and recreation.

Army psychiatrists also developed some effective, short-term treatments for those who needed care. Colonel Frederick Hanson, a military psychiatrist, helped to train other doctors in what he called "first-aid psychiatry." The effectiveness of the methods used during wartime, especially brief but intense psychotherapy, profoundly influenced psychiatry. People were eager to see if similar methods could improve mental health care in America, and they asked the government to support mental health research and promising new treatments.

A new emphasis on funding

In 1946, the year after the war ended, Congress passed the Mental Health Act, establishing the National Institute of Mental Health, which was directed "to improve the mental health of the people of the United States." Congress allocated funding for research and to support state and local programs designed to improve mental health services. Grants were made to universities and other facilities that trained doctors, nurses, and others who worked in mental health fields.

In 1950, the government took another step that put mental illness on a more equal footing with other medical conditions. An amendment to the federal Social Security Act provided funds to the states for people who had become disabled by mental illness. Those who could prove that their condition prevented them from being able to support themselves could receive public assistance through the social security system.

State governments also took action. In 1950, a report by the Council of State Governments, which represented the nation's governors, discussed the need to renovate and improve public mental hospitals. It also discussed ways in which preventive programs and other community care might reduce the number of people in state institutions.

Criticism of institutions

For decades, people had been criticizing state mental institutions. In 1908, *A Mind That Found Itself*, a book by former mental patient Clifford Whittingham Beers, shocked many Americans. A graduate of Yale University, Beers had spent several years in mental hospitals after attempting suicide and being diagnosed with manic-depressive illness. In his book, he criticized the care he had received, the insensitive, untrained attendants working in the institutions, and the "lax system of supervision."

Determined to help others, in 1909 Beers founded the National Committee for Mental Hygiene, which was reorganized as the National Association for Mental Health in 1950. The goal of the organization was to educate the public about conditions in mental institutions and advocate changes that would help the mentally ill and their families.

Through the efforts of Beers and others, more Americans became aware that filthy, abusive mental asylums were not a thing of the past. By the 1950s, conditions in many state mental hospitals were grim. Buildings had been neglected for

Former mental patient Clifford Whittingham Beers criticized the horrific conditions in state mental institutions in his book published in 1908.

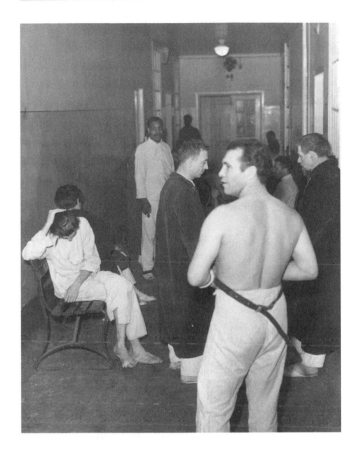

decades. Investigators who visited state hospitals reported seeing mentally ill people wandering the halls moaning or screaming. Some were nearly naked or wore clothing soaked with urine or excrement. Many were kept in restraints for many hours during the day as well as at night.

Along with the dingy, run-down buildings, hospital staffs were criticized. Low budgets meant that many hired to work as attendants in mental institutions had little or no training. Often, there were too few staff members to care for patients properly. In some cases, staff members were allowed to treat patients arbitrarily, without plan or supervision.

Critics also attacked treatments that were ineffective or even harmful. During the 1920s and

1930s, for example, Dr. Henry Cotton, head of a state hospital in New Jersey, believed that infections could cause mental illness. He performed numerous operations on patients, removing their tonsils and teeth in order to prevent these supposed infections. No scientific evidence supported Cotton's methods, but no one in the hospital system challenged his decisions.

At other mental hospitals, patients were intentionally infected with malaria, typhoid, and other diseases in order to bring on a high fever. Some physicians believed that extreme fevers might reduce mental symptoms, but again there was no strong evidence to support these treatments. Investigations also revealed that large numbers of lobotomies had been performed, many of them on people whose main symptoms were anxiety, not those of a psychotic illness.

Scathing publicity

There were countless reports of patient abuse and cases in which people languished in institutions for years, showing no improvement or deteriorating. Studies showed that people institutionalized for many years tended to grow more dependent, and lost contact with their families and communities when they were confined far from home.

To gain support for the mentally ill, advocates publicized shameful hospital conditions and patient abuses, with help from aroused mass media. In 1937, journalist Albert Deutsch wrote a highly praised book about the history of the treatment of the mentally ill in America. He went on to write regular newspaper articles on the subject, enlisting many supporters to the cause of reform.

During the 1940s, Deutsch further investigated mental hospitals and published his findings in a series of scathing articles, illustrated with dis-

Journalist Albert Deutsch published articles condemning poor conditions and patient abuses in mental hospitals. Deutsch's work helped gain support for the mentally ill and encouraged reform of mental institutions.

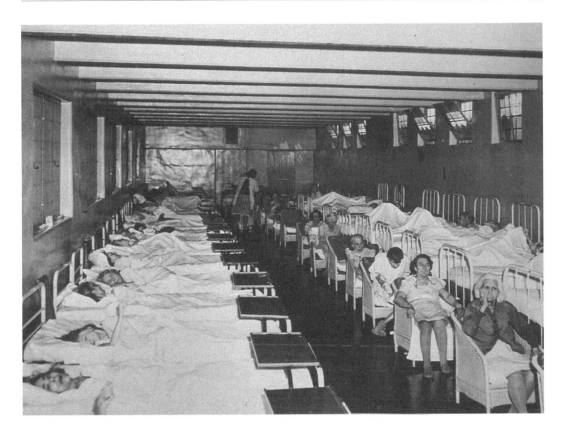

tressing photographs. Of a Detroit facility, he wrote, "I have seen animals better treated and more comfortably housed in zoos." Deutsch decried the overcrowding and understaffing he had witnessed and noted that in some places, patients remained in bed during the daytime because there was not enough clothing to go around. He found that many physicians and staff members seemed genuinely concerned about their patients but lacked the resources to give them adequate care.

In 1948, Deutsch published *The Shame of the States*, arousing still more public support for reforming mental facilities. The book described ways in which state hospitals could be vastly improved, but it also supported the idea of developing psychiatric clinics integrated in the community.

Rows of beds and chairs crowd the mental illness ward at Camarillo State Hospital in California. Overcrowding and understaffing were commonplace in many mental institutions across America.

At the same time, the popular magazine *Life* also publicized the problems of mental institutions in a long article by Albert Maisel called "Bedlam 1946." Calling the institutions "a shame and a disgrace," Maisel said that they were used to jail rather than cure people. The article was widely read and discussed and sparked many editorials recommending mental hospital reform.

Former patients continued to share their experiences. One of them was Marie Balter, who had spent eighteen years in a mental institution, where she was mistakenly diagnosed as a schizophrenic and given medications that made her real problem, a type of depression, worse. Years passed before a new doctor realized that she needed a different prescription. After being discharged from the hospital in 1966, Balter built a new life by earning a master's degree, then working in the mental health field, eventually becoming director of community affairs at Danvers State Hospital in Massachusetts.

More reports surfaced of people confined against their will, some of whom managed to escape and tell their stories. Mae Neustadt, born in 1899, had been confined in a state hospital for forty years, yet apparently had never been insane. She described years of being forced to "walk back and forth with a heavy iron polisher, polishing an already polished floor, and if I stopped for a few seconds to rest, I was struck in the face by the attendant and told to keep polishing until I was told to stop." Neustadt lived in fear of a lobotomy, electrical shocks, and other drastic treatments.

Support for community-based care

Americans, having read the stories and seen the photographs, pressed government leaders for action. Added momentum came via the civil rights movement of the 1950s and 1960s, which increased public awareness of the problems of black Americans. Other minority groups, including the handicapped and the mentally ill, benefited from the heightened public awareness.

A growing movement, supported by government, mental health professionals, and many citizens, favored releasing mental patients into the community where they could participate in life as fully as possible. The emerging campaign, called the community mental health movement, was not entirely new. Throughout history, various individuals had suggested that helping people within their communities might be better than confining them in institutions.

Developing outpatient psychiatric clinics

In 1909, psychiatrist Adolf Meyer outlined the basic principles of community mental health treatment. Called the dean of American psychiatry, Meyer directed the first clinic to be part of a university medical school and hospital, the Henry Phipps Psychiatric Clinic at Johns Hopkins University in Baltimore. Called an outpatient clinic, this facility saw patients on a regular basis, more or less frequently depending on their problems. Doctors at the clinic dispensed medication, conducted psychotherapy sessions, and evaluated the need for hospitalization during periods of severe symptoms. Meyer thought that these kinds of clinics could oversee the care of released mental patients. Supporters hoped to see outpatient clinics replace the poorly run state and private institutions that now haunted the American conscience.

During the 1950s, every state had begun to develop some kind of community program. Local communities were encouraged and sometimes given financial help to set up such services.

Psychiatrist Adolf Meyer directed the first outpatient clinic for the mentally ill. The clinic conducted psychotherapy sessions, dispensed medication, and evaluated the need for hospitalization.

About thirteen hundred outpatient psychiatric clinics were in operation by the mid-1950s, according to a survey conducted by the National Institute of Mental Health.

With the Health Amendments Act of 1955, Congress laid the groundwork for pilot community mental health programs in communities throughout America. The act also established the Joint Commission on Mental Illness and Health (JCMIH), which conducted the first nationwide survey of mental illness in the United States.

A new vision

In 1960, the commission made recommendations based on the needs they had identified. Its report, called *Action for Mental Health*, pointed out that funding for mental health programs had always lagged behind that for other medical problems. The commission blamed this inequality in part on unfair public perceptions of mental illness—for example, that it was often not recognized as illness and that the behavior of the mentally ill frightened and upset people. It also pointed out that the mentally ill often suffer from social isolation, and discussed ways to upgrade care in state hospitals as well as the potential benefits of community mental health centers.

Supporters of community programs described their vision of mental health centers. Anthony Celebrezze, secretary of health, education, and welfare, said in 1962:

> Such centers . . . would be close to the patient's home, and would provide preventive, early diagnostic, and outpatient and inpatient treatment, and transitional and rehabilitative services. They would include psychiatric units in general hospitals, thereby providing the patient with the opportunity of being treated within his community. . . . These facilities . . . could provide patients with a continuity of care not now available.

Among the services Celebrezze and others recommended were diagnosis, treatment, inpatient care, outpatient care, day or night programs, sheltered workshops (supervised jobs), and rehabilitation.

Comprehensive services

In 1963, based on JCMIH recommendations and with strong support from President Kennedy, Congress passed laws including the Mental Health Centers Act. The Mental Health Centers Act enabled communities to apply for federal and state grants that could be used to construct and staff community-based treatment centers. These centers were to include five basic departments: facilities for inpatient care and for partial hospitalization, outpatient services (therapy and counseling), emergency services for people in crisis, and consultation and education services.

Anthony Celebrezze, former secretary of health, education, and welfare, advocated the development of community mental health centers.

These last services showed a strong focus on the prevention of mental disorders. During this era, people were looking closely at how the whole environment, including the community, could affect an individual's mental health. Social ills such as poverty or growing up in high-crime areas were correlated with increased rates of mental illnesses. Mental health center staffs were mandated to consult with and educate members of the community likely to come into contact with citizens suffering from or at risk for mental illnesses. The clergy, police officers, day care centers staffs, teachers, welfare agency staffs, and visiting nurses, among others, were on the front lines of the prevention effort, daily in contact with people who might need help but be reluctant to receive counseling or visit a psychiatrist. Members of the community could attend educational programs at the local community mental health center to help them cope with the mental and emotional problems of the center's clients.

They could also consult with staff members if they needed help to solve mental health problems that arose in their work.

To help people function better and use the resources in the community, the centers sponsored programs on such topics as parenting and nutrition. Those who came for counseling often had other needs, such as for education, employment, or physical health care, that aggravated their mental problems. Working with a network of community agencies, center staffs tried to give people comprehensive help that would lead to real improvements in daily life.

As the pendulum swung clearly toward integrating the mentally ill into society, states passed new laws that supported the community mental health effort. One such law stated that patients should be treated in the least restrictive environment possible. This meant that hospitals were obligated to offer patients considered capable of leaving the hospital setting other, less confining, treatment. Thus, in addition to mental health centers, communities developed halfway houses, sheltered workshops, day treatment programs, and vocational training programs for formerly institutionalized mental patients. Outpatient clinics helped clients monitor their medications and provided counseling on a regular basis.

An emphasis on prevention

Community mental health programs continued to grow in the early 1970s. With strong political support, federal officials conducted more mental health studies and proposed expanded services. In 1978, President Jimmy Carter appointed the President's Commission on Mental Health, which reported on the need for continuing the community-based approach, with outreach programs that would actively involve mental health

President Jimmy Carter supported the community mental health movement. His President's Commission on Mental Health stressed the importance of prevention and the need to help people during times of crisis.

workers in the community—for example, in schools, recreational centers, and welfare agencies.

The President's Commission had emphasized the importance of prevention and the need to help people during times of crisis, such as unemployment, marital conflict, retirement, and mourning, when people are more vulnerable to stress and illness. Some efforts, such as parent education and drug education in the schools, were geared toward primary prevention, aimed at preventing the occurrence of mental illnesses. Secondary prevention, aimed at detecting and treating problems as quickly as possible, emphasized early intervention. This might include identifying a toddler with learning disorders and helping the child and family as soon as possible, or counseling people through a job loss or death in the family. Tertiary prevention efforts were designed to rehabilitate a person so that future complications were reduced. An example would be services to someone who had just left a mental institution, through regular outpatient care and perhaps family counseling.

Defining mental health

As people discussed the idea of preventing mental illness and promoting mental health, they struggled to define mental health. The World Health Organization has said that health is "a state of complete physical, mental, and social well being and not merely the absence of disease or infirmity." Funk and Wagnall's encyclopedia defines mental health as a state of "psychological well-being and self-acceptance, capacity to love and relate to others, ability to work productively, willingness to behave in a way that brings personal satisfaction without encroaching upon the rights of others." Other definitions embellish these ideas, saying that healthy individuals are at ease with themselves and their environment, have a sense of security and belonging, and are able to pursue reasonable goals, using their talents and capabilities in a positive way.

The new emphasis on health rather than illness and on prevention rather than cure led to new ways of looking at the mentally ill. It was hoped that by emphasizing health, in neighborhood settings that conducted a wide variety of educational and treatment programs, people would be more inclined to seek help. The government and various mental health organizations worked to increase public understanding of mental illness and reduce its stigma. Public service announcements on radio and television described typical signs of mental illness and described ways to find help.

On the whole, the mood of the 1960s was typified by a less judgmental attitude toward the mentally ill as well as others who were different or atypical. This went along with the social mood that prevailed during the 1960s, in which authority figures and old ideas were challenged, while individual freedom was celebrated.

The community mental health movement enjoyed much support, but people also voiced concerns. Some experts feared that the most critically and chronically ill patients were getting lost in the shuffle, not receiving the care they needed. Others said that more overall planning was needed, along with research to determine to what extent the goals of community programs were being met. As time went on, it became clear that the drive to release patients into the community and the focus on prevention and wellness, rather than mental illness, were achieving mixed results.

4

Beyond the Open Door

THE COMMUNITY MENTAL health movement achieved some of its broad and idealistic goals. More people, including low-income Americans, had access to mental health services. A number of problems were identified earlier than they had been in the past. Legislation reinforced the rights of mental patients. Yet some problems persisted, and new ones resulted from the massive release of patients from state mental institutions.

Dissenting voices

From the start, a number of people had voiced reservations about the community mental health approach. In 1954, Kenneth R. Appel, the president of the American Psychiatric Association, had stressed the need for nationwide, long-term planning. Appel and others thought such planning was needed in order to determine which mental health problems needed solutions, what resources were needed throughout the nation, and how priorities were to be set.

Other experts, usually medical doctors, objected to the strong bias toward psychological therapies shown by government task forces and mental health care planners. They worried that

(Opposite page) A mental institution patient peers through the window of a door in her room. For many institutionalized individuals, the transition from hospital to community can be very frightening. Community mental health programs helped many people but also left many others without badly needed continuous care.

71

little attention was being paid to biological aspects of mental illness or to studies showing that some mental illnesses seemed to be rooted in biochemical imbalances. They objected to a report by one government task force that said that mental illnesses were not illnesses but social disorders, and as such, did not require medical attention. A group of psychiatrists sent a dissenting letter to the authors of the report citing studies that showed certain patients with severe psychoses did not improve without medical care in a hospital setting.

A fashionable movement?

Journalist Albert Deutsch, known for his earlier exposés of the problems of state institutions, also warned that some of the ideas about mental health might be "ambiguous" and "fleeting." In a 1956 article in the journal *Mental Hygiene*, Deutsch said that he feared people might be getting caught up in a fashionable movement without making sure there was a scientific basis for these ideas. He also warned that patients who truly needed hospitalization might be abandoned. Deutsch was among those who warned against hastily embracing something new that might turn out to generate problems as well as benefits.

Others pointed out that concepts like "mental health," "community mental health," and "prevention" were unclear. Different people might define these concepts quite differently. Because the federal government was giving funds directly to local communities, rather than to the states, local centers had a great deal of discretion in designing their own mental health programs. On the one hand, this might allow them to better address the specific needs of their communities. But it also caused some confusion when deciding who was responsible for mental patients who had previously been cared for by the state. Critics of the community mental health approach worried that nobody was clearly accountable for the fate of the patients who left state hospitals.

In 1968, Congress said that federally funded centers must add new programs for children, the elderly, and people who abused drugs or alcohol. Yet funding for community programs was dwindling. Large federal health insurance programs for the elderly and the poor had taken effect in the early 1960s. The war in Vietnam also escalated during these years, consuming millions of tax dollars. Many community mental health centers were never funded; others were planned but not built.

Some positive results

As community mental health programs developed, people did see some benefits. Among the positive results was a heightened awareness of the importance of mental health. Attitudes became less judgmental, and some of the stigma against mental illness seemed to diminish.

The community mental health movement heightened society's understanding of mental illnesses. Therapies like family counseling have helped people learn to communicate and resolve interpersonal conflicts.

People also learned more about promoting their own mental health. There was more interest in how people interact. Instead of focusing on what was "wrong" with an individual, say a spouse or a child who was troubled, therapists looked at how the marriage or the family functioned. This approach placed less blame on individuals. It led to promising therapies that helped people to communicate and resolve interpersonal conflicts more effectively.

These approaches also considered a person's immediate environment. For example, if a child was having behavioral problems, a therapist might decide it made more sense to work with the parents and teachers rather than directly with the child, offering parents and teachers new skills to use in dealing with that child outside of therapy.

As people became more willing to express emotions and admit various problems, the num-

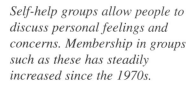

Self-help groups allow people to discuss personal feelings and concerns. Membership in groups such as these has steadily increased since the 1970s.

ber of support and self-help groups increased. People struggling with any number of problems—the illness of a loved one, widowhood, depression, alcoholism—could meet and share their feelings and concerns. The number and types of various groups also increased and memberships rose steadily from the 1970s, to the present day.

Community mental health programs improved access to treatment for more people than ever before. Clients, as they were called, could receive treatment and learn about mental health in places that were more conveniently located in or near their neighborhoods. People could attend education or self-help groups run by trained professionals. Those in the midst of a crisis could find a center open twenty-four hours a day for emergencies. Till then, their only option had been to go to hospital emergency rooms, which might lack psychiatrists or other mental health professionals. Many people benefited from the comprehensive services that were developed at some centers. But some critics warned that mental health centers were trying to do too much.

A psychiatric nurse who worked in a mental health center in West Virginia during the mid-1970s says, "At that time, we were pretty free to develop programs on our own, whatever we thought might benefit the community. There was a lot of enthusiasm and a desire to meet many needs, but not much clear direction."

In some places, programs for formerly institutionalized mental patients were carefully developed. Hospitals coordinated efforts with community mental health programs. In Vermont, a research project measured the results of such programs. They found that if people with severe mental illnesses had proper follow-up care and a wide range of services to meet their varied needs, many could indeed live in the community rather

A man receives computer training at the Fountain House Day Care and Job Training Center in New York. Occupational therapy, coupled with mental health care, has allowed many formerly institutionalized people to make the transition from hospital to community.

than in hospitals. Most of the patients in the study had a diagnosis of schizophrenia, had been ill for an average of sixteen years, and had no immediate families or other support systems. Many also had physical disabilities.

To ease these patients' passage from institution to community, the staffs at the hospitals used group therapy sessions, vocational counseling, occupational therapy, and self-help groups. The patients' medications were monitored carefully to make sure they were using the most effective drugs at the right dosages.

Once the patients left the hospital, the community mental health center staffs went to work immediately. Patients were either placed in halfway houses or scheduled for regular outpatient clinic visits. Staff members helped them to find jobs and made sure they received other needed services.

An Ohio man who moved from a psychiatric hospital into the community describes his positive experience. During his early twenties, he had been diagnosed with paranoid schizophrenia. By age thirty-four, he had been hospitalized four times and had gone through several jobs and a divorce. In 1975, he entered a day care treatment program sponsored by a community mental health center.

The structured living arrangements and supervision, along with individual and group therapy and medication, helped him to cope with his mental illness. He was eventually able to live in an apartment and to maintain a job. He says, "I learned the importance of getting help as soon as I think I'm in trouble. I've had to come into the twenty-four-hour-clinic at night a few times for help. I still take medication, come to group sessions, and see a therapist monthly. But I'm making it."

There are other examples of seriously ill people who were successfully treated by community mental health centers. But many experts have

A group of mentally ill men gathers in the dining hall of their day care center. These centers provide essential services to formerly institutionalized individuals, including structured living arrangements, group therapy, and medication distribution.

concluded that such programs were most helpful to people with less severe problems. Historian Gerald Grob writes, "Community mental health centers from their origins began to deal with new categories of individuals with emotional disturbances rather than severe mental disorders." Many of the people being served were newcomers to the mental health system rather than people who had been discharged by hospitals or those who were likely to end up there.

Problems in the system

A social worker who worked at a mental health center near Columbus, Ohio, for eight years describes the growth of a much larger "detection net" for mental problems. She says:

> As the center and its staff became more visible in the community, more problems were identified as needing mental health care. People came to the centers who would probably not have sought counseling in the past. These were mainly people with emotional and personal problems, not severe illnesses. Some people who came to meetings at the center seemed to come because they were lonely.

During the 1970s, critics pointed out serious shortcomings in the evolving mental health care system. In an article called "The Community Mental Health Center: Does It Treat Patients?", Donald G. Langsley, president of the American Psychiatric Association, said that the programs were not reaching the primary population they had been designed to serve, namely formerly institutionalized patients. Instead, said Langsley, community mental health centers were focusing on "counseling and crisis intervention for predictable problems of living."

Langsley pointed out that the centers hired far more social workers and psychologists than psychiatrists. As medical doctors, the latter were more apt to have experience and training in serious mental illnesses. Yet many mental health center staffs believed it was vital to help people with less serious problems, supported by the theories behind prevention and crisis intervention. During the 1960s, many people had begun to view mental illness as a continuum. Some believed that certain problems of living and emotional distress could lead to future mental illnesses. Often, clear distinctions were not made between severe mental illnesses and less serious problems.

Inevitably, mental health centers devoting themselves to the latter had fewer resources to deal with seriously ill people, whose more complex, more difficult problems required larger amounts of time, money, and other resources, as well as ongoing help with daily living.

A gap in services emerges

Some states, such as California, adopted policies urging community centers to work hand in hand with state hospitals, but programs varied greatly within that state. Some states had no clear-cut policies. Individual centers developed an array of plans to deal with the seriously ill.

In 1979, Jimmy Carter's President's Commission on Mental Health expressed concern that mental health centers were not meeting the many needs of seriously mentally ill people, whom they referred to as "the type most likely to spend time in a State Hospital." The commission said:

> We have heard of woefully inadequate follow-up mental health and general medical care. And we have seen evidence that half the people released from large mental hospitals are being readmitted within a year of discharge.

Between 1955 and 1980, the number of people in state mental hospitals declined from more than 550,000 to about 125,000. States closed down

A woman begs for money in front of her community-based home. Opponents of the community mental health movement contend that many patients who are released from mental institutions require more care and supervision than they receive in their communities.

some mental hospitals and reduced the size of others. Hospital stays also tended to be shorter. For every ten state mental hospital beds that were eliminated, there were only about three publicly funded replacements in, for example, group homes or supervised apartments. Ex-patients often had nowhere to go.

Historian Gerald Grob says that the kinds of patients being released from hospitals also changed. The patients who had been discharged during the 1960s were mostly older people who had been in institutions for at least a few years. These people usually went to places where they received ongoing care or some supervision and seemed to do fairly well.

However, during the 1970s, younger, more mobile people were released into the community. The baby boom of 1945–1961 produced the largest young adult population in history, which made for larger numbers of young mentally ill people. Says Grob, "The young adult mentally ill exhibited aggressiveness, volatility, and were noncompliant. . . . They lacked functional and adaptive skills." Many also had problems with drugs, alcohol, or both. Frequently they could not maintain a job or residence. Many became homeless.

These patients also tended to use mental health services in an erratic fashion. Caregivers' efforts were frustrated by patients who showed up during a crisis, received care for a while, then disappeared again. They often ignored medical advice, arousing anger and distrust on the part of mental health professionals unprepared for interrupted therapy or uncooperative clients.

Lack of follow-up care

Clearly, many former hospital patients did not receive adequate follow-up care. One reason, cited previously, was that funding dwindled in the late 1960s and 1970s. Inflation rose and the U.S. economy weakened. Public and political interest in funding mental health centers decreased, and Congress urged the states to take more responsibility for financing their own programs.

Congress had envisioned funding about 2,000 centers across the nation. By 1970, 274 were operating; by 1980, only 754 centers were receiving funding. Between 1963 and 1968, Congress released only 40 percent of the money it had originally committed to fund community mental health centers. Lacking funding, many community centers never set up aftercare facilities that would have served former hospital patients. In many areas, a shortage of psychiatrists and other professionals was also never remedied.

By necessity, states developed their own programs to house former mental patients. About thirteen states tried placing them in homes with families. However, these home-care programs met with resistance from other residents in the community, and they were difficult to supervise. Halfway houses also served as places for patients to stay immediately after leaving the hospital and before moving into the community. A lack of funding and the short-term nature of these facilities led halfway houses to become less popular by the end of the 1970s.

Extensive services needed

Research during the 1950s and 1960s had predicted that numerous problems might occur if seriously ill people did not receive continuing, comprehensive services after leaving the hospital. In California, researchers had assessed the results of hospital versus clinic treatment for groups of psychiatric patients. They found only 57 of 504 people in one group were realistic candidates for outpatient treatment in clinics. Of these 57, only 6 were accepted by the clinic as outpatients, and only 2 kept their appointments. The researchers concluded that patients needed extensive social services and help in various areas of life—jobs and housing, for example—or they would not succeed in outpatient treatment.

Another group of researchers at Ohio State University compared the results of hospital care, home care in which patients received placebo medications with no active ingredients, and home care in which patients received genuine medication. The results, reported in a 1967 book called *Schizophrenics in the Community*, showed that the home care group receiving genuine medication improved the most. However, Dr. Benjamin Pasamanick, who led the study, pointed out that at the time of the study, community mental health programs lacked the services that would make such care feasible. Pasamanick and his team found that programs for severely and chronically ill patients were not as comprehensive as they were intended to be.

The system falters

President Carter's commission suggested ways to resolve these problems in its 1980 Mental Health Systems Act. The Carter administration also proposed the National Plan for the Chronically Mentally Ill, which would have blended federal disability programs with the mental health care system in order to coordinate care for people with chronic mental illnesses. But this act was passed just before the 1980 presidential election, which Carter lost to Ronald Reagan.

Under President Reagan, the Omnibus Budget Reconciliation Act became law in 1981, authorizing cuts in all areas of the federal budget. It radically changed the ways in which federal mental health programs were funded. Now, states could receive block sums of money to use for anything from mental health centers to substance abuse programs. States did not have to comply with many guidelines in order to receive these grants. Most of the Mental Health Systems Act of 1980 was cancelled under the new legislation.

Increasingly, patients did not receive follow-up care because they dropped out of treatment. Some chose to stop; others lacked either the ability to follow through or caring families or friends to make sure they kept appointments or took their prescription drugs. A number of patients stopped taking their medications because they disliked their side effects; some common antipsychotic drugs caused, for example, dry mouth and involuntary twitching in addition to their beneficial effects. Others simply could not figure out what to do once they were on their own. As a result, during the late 1970s, statistics from the National Institute of Mental Health showed that two of every three patients released from a mental hospital were later readmitted.

Patients' rights issues

Legal issues also affected the treatment of seriously mentally ill people. The 1960s and 1970s witnessed a strong societal concern with individual civil liberties, including patients' rights. More people challenged the idea of mental illness itself. Some contended that a repressive, sick society was the problem, not the people labeled as mentally ill. There was a growing movement to "live and let live," accepting more differences and tolerating behavior once labeled deviant.

The involuntary commitment of people to mental institutions came under fire. Like many other nations, the United States had laws regulating the commitment process, which enabled public officials or relatives to commit people to treatment or mental institutions over their objections. But these regulations tended to be broad and allowed people to be committed fairly easily.

Now, critics argued that courts and health professionals should not have the right to deprive people of their physical freedom or administer treatment against their will. States narrowed the grounds upon which people could be committed to a hospital or a doctor's care. Lawyers also filed suits on patients' behalf to force institutions confining people to guarantee them an adequate level of treatment and care.

In most places, the standard test for involuntary commitment became whether or not people were

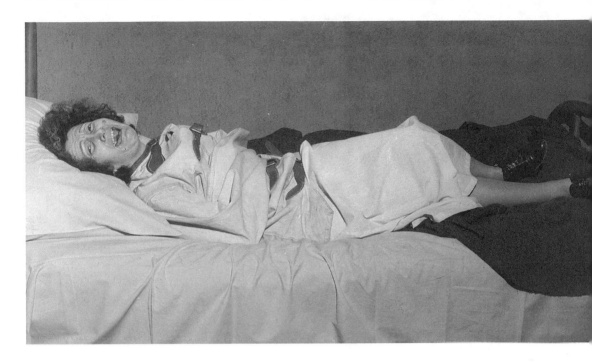

a danger to themselves or others. To guard a patient's rights, commitment hearings were held in a timely manner, usually within forty-eight hours. At that time a judge heard testimony by psychiatrists and others in order to decide whether a commitment was legally justified. Laws further limited the length of time one could be committed. These kinds of legal decisions seem to reflect the belief that hospital treatment is less desirable than treatment in the community.

The end result was that during the 1980s many seriously and chronically mentally ill people became more visible. Whereas in years past, they would have been institutionalized, now they were often left to their own devices. Many had nowhere to go, adding to the increasing number of homeless mentally ill people on the streets of America, a problem that persists to this day.

Laws regulating the commitment process were often broad and allowed public officials or relatives to forcibly commit people to mental institutions.

5

Aftercare and Involuntary Commitment

ALTHOUGH MANY PEOPLE with serious mental illnesses have moved successfully from hospitals to the community, thousands have not. By the early 1990s, it was estimated that more than 200,000 mentally ill people lived on the street. Experts guess that between 25 and 33 percent of the homeless have a severe mental illness, while another third may have alcohol and drug problems. Some of these people arouse pity and concern. They may appear confused, panicky, sad, or unable to meet their own needs. Others have made news headlines by assaulting and harassing neighbors.

The homeless mentally ill

(Opposite page) A homeless woman shuffles along a busy sidewalk. Experts believe that approximately 25 to 33 percent of all homeless individuals suffer from severe mental disorders. Balancing the rights of people with mental illness and other residents of the community is not always easy.

In a column called "Sick and Cheated," journalist Bob Herbert wrote:

> For years we have been told that the massive discharge of patients from mental institutions would not be harmful because the patients would receive the services they needed from facilities in the community. This has been a fantasy. If you don't believe it, take a walk through the streets or the parks of New York. Or take a ride on the subway.

Increasing numbers of homeless people are afflicted with mental illnesses that keep them from functioning in society. These individuals can frequently be found wandering the streets or sitting for hours on park benches.

Says Dr. E. Fuller Torrey, "The *new* homeless look vacantly off into space, talk amicably to nearby trees, or clutch their bags around them on a park bench as they look out at a world full of unnamed terrors."

Citizens and public officials disagree about what to do. They are unsure whether the homeless mentally ill should be jailed, placed in hospitals, or given treatment. They are equally uncertain about how to respond when someone refuses help.

In 1987, with thousands of homeless mentally ill, New York City decided that these people should have medical care. That October, as winter approached, city officials picked up people and took them to Bellevue Hospital for mental evaluations. One of those committed was Joyce Brown, who called herself Billie Boggs. During the previous year, Brown had lived on the street, where people saw her urinating on the sidewalk, screaming at passersby, and burning dollar bills. Angry at being committed, Brown sued the city.

The case drew nationwide attention. At that time, laws in New York, like those in many states, required that people be both mentally ill and a danger to themselves or others to justify commitment. The American Civil Liberties Union (ACLU) and others argued that Brown had a right both to live on the street and to resist treatment. They said she posed no danger to herself or others and accused city officials of rounding up homeless people in order to clean up New York's streets and please wealthier citizens. Mayor Ed Koch and his supporters disagreed, saying that cities have a duty to help people who cannot care for themselves.

Early in 1988, Brown won her lawsuit and was released from the hospital, but that decision was

Joyce Brown (center), a homeless mentally ill woman who called herself Billie Boggs, was involuntarily committed to Bellevue Hospital in New York City in 1987. Brown sued the city for its action, claiming it was her right to live on the street and to resist treatment.

overturned in 1989. In *Boggs v. New York City Health and Hospitals Corporation*, the appeals court agreed with city officials that people who cannot or who refuse to take care of their basic needs for food, shelter, clothing, or health care can be considered dangerous to themselves. Yet people disagree about how to define "dangerous." Steven Sanders, chairman of the Mental Health Committee in New York, said that, in his view, "People don't necessarily have to be dangling from the Brooklyn Bridge or threatening people with an ice pick."

Coping with those who pose a threat

Studies show that mentally ill people tend to be less violent than the rest of society. But those who commit crimes or frighten others often make news headlines. In a 1990 article, author Joan Phillips described how she and others living in a seventeen-story apartment building were terrorized by a woman in her thirties with a long history of mental illness. The woman's parents had cared for her, but after they died she stopped taking her medication and began filling her apartment with bags of garbage. She attacked people going to the laundry room, in the halls, and outside the building. Police were called many times, but were unable to have the woman committed for very long. She had done nothing sufficiently dangerous, they explained.

The difficulty of proving that people are dangerous to themselves or others may prevent families from having members committed who need care, until they have already hurt someone or are clearly about to do so. In *Madness in the Streets*, authors Virginia Armat and Rael Jean Isaac describe one of these complex cases. A couple had a mentally ill son who had been hospitalized thirty times. He showed improvement and moved into his own apartment, planning to join a work program. One evening, while his mother was visiting, he attacked her from behind and fractured her skull. It turned out that he had stopped taking his medication six weeks previously when his doctor let him switch from injections to pills.

After the mother recovered, she and her husband were shocked when their son's attorney suggested he *not* use an insanity defense, which, said the attorney, could put him in a mental hospital for life. The parents feared that unless their son were hospitalized, he would not take care of himself and might become violent again. At the trial, the attorney plea-bargained, and the son was convicted of assault with a deadly weapon. Released after six years in prison, he again stopped taking his antipsychotic medication.

A dangerous mix

There have been other cases in which people formerly diagnosed as mentally ill committed violent crimes. These people had left treatment or fallen through the cracks of both the criminal justice and mental health systems. Studies showed that in the early 1990s, about 10 to 15 percent of the inmates in state prisons—nearly 100,000 people—had serious mental illnesses.

Among the people who have been identified as being mentally ill years before they committed serious crimes are Sylvia Seegrist, who shot ten people at a shopping center near Philadelphia; Herbert Mullin, who killed thirteen people at random near San Francisco; Laurie Dann, who killed six children at an elementary school outside Chicago; and John Hinckley, who tried to assassinate President Ronald Reagan. Cases like these and that of Kevin McKiever, a mentally ill man who fatally stabbed a thirty-year-old woman one morning while she was walking her dogs, have

John Hinckley was diagnosed as being mentally ill prior to his attempted assassination of President Ronald Reagan.

A homeless man sleeps on a city sidewalk. Such spectacles sometimes cause the general public to criticize the government for not providing aid and treatment.

increased pressure from the public and the courts to improve the process of confining people who are likely to hurt others.

Changing laws

Throughout America, states have been reexamining their commitment laws. In 1994, the New York State legislature considered new bills that make it easier to force mentally ill people into treatment or have them committed. Legislators, patient advocates, and civil liberties advocates worked on these bills. One sponsor, state senator Frank Padavan, said, "The general public is pained by individuals who they can see need help but are not getting it. They criticize government for not doing anything but they don't realize the constraints government is working under."

Luis D. Marcos, commissioner of New York City's Department of Mental Health, Mental Retardation, and Alcoholism Services supports laws that would place former mental patients under court order to either take medication and get counseling or return to the hospital. "Most patients, [when] a judge orders them to do something, they will try to comply. It also forces the clinicians, the clinics, the hospitals to do something when the patient doesn't show up."

States have passed other laws to deal with these kinds of problems. By 1993, twenty-six states required mental patients to comply with a "sensible out-patient program." One New York law allows police to detain someone for up to forty-eight hours if behavior dangerous to themselves or others is a result of alcohol or drugs. Another change, proposed in various states, would allow nurses and social workers, as well as doctors, to send homeless people for mental evaluations if their behavior indicated that mental illness was a likely possibility.

Gratitude and alarm

Former patients have also spoken out about the issue. Some express gratitude that they were forced to receive care. They claim that at the time of their commitment, they were not thinking clearly enough to make sound decisions and might have committed suicide or done something they would later regret. Musician Philip H. Dolinsky, diagnosed with schizophrenia, was committed in 1988 after being arrested for throwing garbage cans on the tracks at a railroad station. After nine months at a hospital, Dolinsky moved to a special housing program. He now takes medication to control his symptoms and pursues his career. In an interview with writer Lisa Foderaro, Dolinsky stated, "Involuntary commitment saved my life."

Other patients describe negative, frightening experiences and resent having been forcibly injected with medications or strapped down. The potential for abuses worries many, including the

ACLU, which has opposed changes that would make it easier to commit people.

People who support broader involuntary commitment laws say that in order to have freedom, a person must be able to think and choose rationally—skills that seriously ill people lack. In "The Mental Health Mess," E. Fuller Torrey writes:

> It would be a great thing if all individuals with schizophrenia and manic-depressive illness could think clearly and understand their need for treatment. Unfortunately, the organ they use for thinking, the brain, is the one that is affected by these diseases. Hence approximately half of all those with serious mental illnesses have little or no insight into their own condition or need for treatment.

Family members say that some laws aimed at protecting the mentally ill actually lead to neglect. State laws vary. The American Bar Association's Commission on Mental and Physical Disability Law found that, as of 1993, the laws in ten states require that people suffer from a grave disability and also be dangerous to themselves or others in order to be committed. In other states, people can be committed if they seem "obviously ill" or seem to "need treatment," giving more discretion to psychiatrists and the courts.

Rethinking the role of mental institutions

Historian Gerald Grob says that after years of rejecting the idea of mental institutions, society now needs to reconsider their role. In *Mental Illness and American Society, 1875–1940*, he writes, "With all of its shortcomings, it was among the few institutions that provided some minimal basic care for persons whose mental and physical conditions—whatever the origins of the conditions—rendered them dependent upon others for their very survival."

In recent decades, therapists and clinics have been sued when patients committed violent acts after discharge or while under treatment. As in any doctor-patient relationship, mental patients traditionally had a right to privacy. Matters discussed in therapy were confidential. But courts have limited such privacy. In the case of *Tarasoff v. Regents of the University of California*, the court said a therapist has a duty to warn those who are in danger from a patient. Some states have also passed laws that make it more difficult for potentially dangerous patients to leave mental hospitals, even for weekend passes. Again, these are complex issues that involve balancing conflicting rights and privileges.

As yet, there is no foolproof way to predict future dangerous behavior. Doctors, especially those in emergency rooms, struggle to make correct decisions. Studies reveal that doctors tend to advise commitment when there is some possibility that the person poses a threat. Scientists are trying to determine the personality traits and social factors that go along with a tendency to commit violent acts. Until more is known, professionals will be forced to make educated judgments, however imperfect, in this area of mental illness, one of the most complex that societies face.

6

Today's Challenges

AS THE TWENTY-FIRST CENTURY approaches, great progress is being made in the study of mental illnesses. The future promises to bring new insights, better treatments, perhaps even cures. At the same time, society continues to wrestle with the personal and social effects of mental illnesses. As in the past, people are trying to balance the rights of the mentally ill with those of others in society.

The quest for causes and cures

Continuing research has produced breakthroughs in understanding the possible causes of mental illnesses. New technology has allowed scientists to study the structure and biochemistry of the brain in far greater detail than ever before. As a result, there is a renewed emphasis on the biological theories of mental illness.

Scientists have found differences in the physical makeup of people with mental disorders. Some people with mental illnesses have abnormal levels of certain blood chemicals or chemicals at the receptor sites of their nerve cells. They may have areas in the brain where messages travel more slowly than they do in nonaffected people.

(Opposite page) Although the future is promising for the study of mental illnesses, millions of people continue to struggle with these disorders on a daily basis.

97

A young boy undergoes computerized axial tomography, usually referred to as a CAT scan. This technology uses X rays to create a detailed picture of an organ's structure, thus allowing doctors and scientists to better understand some of the biological causes of mental illnesses.

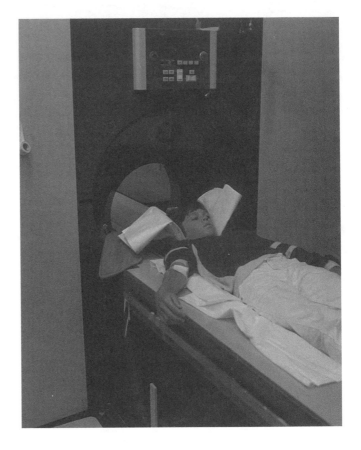

Using computers and other tools, scientists can study brain wave patterns and compare psychotic and normal electrical activity. Computerized axial tomography (called a CAT or CT scan) became available in 1971. Using a series of X rays directed at cross-sections of a patient's body, the resulting patterns are analyzed with a computer. The patterns give a detailed picture of an organ's structure but cannot describe its functioning, that is, its chemical processes or use of energy.

Magnetic resonance imaging (MRI), positron emission tomography (PET), and brain electrical activity mapping (BEAM) have also increased knowledge of the brain. Scientists have developed color-coded maps of brain activity. With PET scans, they study the inside of a living brain and measure the blood flow and chemical activity of cells. This shows how different parts of the brain use energy. Scientists have identified abnormal brain metabolism in people who suffer from dementia, epilepsy, schizophrenia, and mood disorders.

A number of scientists have focused on schizophrenia. They have found that people with schizophrenia do not use the naturally occurring chemical dopamine in a normal way. Dopamine is a neurotransmitter, a chemical that helps to transmit messages across nerve cells. Schizophrenics have an abnormally high number of dopamine receptors in their brains. Using PET scans, American scientist Dr. Dean Wong examined dopamine receptors in the brains of living people diagnosed with schizophrenia. He found more of one type of dopamine receptors (called D-2) in people with schizophrenia than in those without. Since the patients in both studies had never taken medications, he concluded that the findings were not due to the effects of drugs. While studying the brain tissue of deceased schizophrenics, German scientists found visible abnormalities in the cells. Scientists now hold schizophrenia to be clearly a disease of the brain.

In studies of autism, a condition in which people withdraw from the world around them and are unable to communicate or empathize normally with others, scientists have found less activity in the right halves of patients' brains. The right half is the region that controls many aspects of personality including social interaction, emotion, and the emotional aspects of speech.

Zeroing in on physical causes

Based on these findings, some scientists think that, in time, organic, or physical, causes will be found for most or all kinds of mental illnesses.

An autistic man hides his face in frustration after struggling to make his bed. Studies of autism have shown that there is less activity in the right half of the brain, resulting in an inability to communicate.

With more knowledge about what is happening in the brain, care and treatment can be enhanced and more effective medications can be developed. Cosmo Hallstrom, a London psychiatrist, thinks that in the future, drugs may be safer, easier to take, and more pleasant. With fewer problem side effects, it may be possible to increase the doses of medications for more severe symptoms. New drugs may address the underlying causes of mental illness, not just the symptoms. Also being developed are substances to improve withdrawal from drugs and alcohol and reduce the urge to relapse. Much research is being devoted to the study of aging. A growing elderly population, some with organic brain disorders, poses challenges for both the mental health care system and families and nursing homes. Alzheimer's disease has received special attention, as have age-associated memory problems.

Progress in psychological research continues, as scientists learn more about how humans learn

Today, considerable research is being devoted to the study of aging. Individuals suffering from Alzheimer's disease pose challenges to mental health care workers, nursing homes, and families.

and grow, through such processes as information processing, thinking, language, emotions, attitudes, and socializing. Experts think that more people may seek counseling in the future as they learn more about mental health and look for a higher level of well-being in all areas of their lives.

Reaching those who need help

By the 1990s, it was estimated that 75 to 80 percent of patients with major depression, manic-depressive illness, and panic disorder could be treated successfully. The outlook for other disorders has steadily improved, and new treatments are on the horizon.

Even so, many people do not seek treatment. There is still ignorance, fear, and prejudice about mental illness. Some people continue to think that mental problems reflect weakness and that the mentally ill lack willpower or character. People fear being ridiculed and rejected if they are labeled mentally ill. They may also worry about the effect such a diagnosis could have on other areas of life, such as employment or their health insurance.

In its large-scale study of mental illness in America, reported in 1993, the National Institute of Mental Health found that of the fifty-two million adults who suffer from a mental disorder each year, about 28 percent (three out of ten) seek help: 18 percent turn to non–mental health professionals, such as friends, family, or self-help groups; 20 percent turn to the clergy. General physicians, not psychiatrists or other mental health specialists, see the majority of people seeking help.

The community mental health movement fostered ongoing efforts to find people who need help and to deal with mental illness early, often through community outreach and education programs. Go where the patient is, has become a theme in many places. Many people who do not seek help can be found in streets, subway terminals, bus depots, railroad stations, boarding houses, churches, the Salvation Army, and other places. Some cities have mobile psychiatric units that are affiliated with local hospitals and monitor mentally ill people on the street.

The team approach

To help people who have left mental hospitals, innovative aftercare programs have been devised. The goal of these programs is to help people live as normally as possible. Some states assign social workers to regularly visit former patients and help them with housing, day treatment, jobs, and medications. Teams may also deal with the homeless mentally ill.

One program in Michigan uses a comprehensive team approach to help people develop skills they need to function personally, socially, and at work. Teams include a psychiatrist, social worker, nurse, and occupational therapist. They visit patients at home, in the office, and at organized social events held twice a year to see how they are getting along.

Results have been encouraging. Some patients who were used to prolonged hospital stays have not needed to return while working with the team and using foster homes, supervised work programs, and other resources. The number of hospital days needed by these patients fell by more than 70 percent after the first year in the program and more than 90 percent after the third year. By 1994, the program was serving some eighty-five thousand severely ill people in Michigan. The people behind this program attribute its success to continuity of care. Patients have ongoing relationships with the same caregivers, people who are familiar with their history and treatment. There is strong accountability as designated mental health professionals oversee the aftercare process.

In 1985, the Robert Wood Johnson Foundation, a private foundation concerned with health issues, gave nine cities funds to develop pilot programs for chronically mentally ill persons. The goal of the Program on Chronic Mental Illness is to demonstrate effective ways to plan and deliver community care. Experts still believe that most mentally ill people, particularly those who are not also substance abusers, can make this adjustment. The pilot programs have demonstrated effective ways to deliver services and may serve as models for future programs.

Housing the chronically mentally ill

The current trend is for residential care to take place in smaller and more personal settings rather than large institutions. For mentally ill people who cannot live on their own, group homes have

A man troubled by mental illness now lives in an apartment in publicly funded transitional housing. Innovative aftercare programs help formerly institutionalized people locate housing, function in society, and live as normally as possible.

replaced many state institutions. Homes are set up with counselors in residence twenty-four hours a day. Most have strict rules and curfews. They require that residents either attend school, training, or day treatment, or that they have a job, do volunteer work, or are actively looking for work. People take turns with chores, such as cooking. Alcohol and drugs are banned.

Group home care costs about one-third as much per patient per year as confinement in a state hospital, which can cost more than $100,000 a year per person. In 1975, there were 209 group homes nationwide, and by 1990, there were thousands. The supply lags behind the need, however. With 700 group homes, New York City still has a long waiting list.

Frequently, citizens oppose the idea of a group home in their community. Towns have passed zoning laws to prevent the homes from being set up. Citizen groups have hired lawyers to find ways to block them. In *9 Highland Road*, Michael Winerip describes a bitter battle that took place in Glen Cove, New York, over a proposed group home for twelve adults with serious illnesses. In 1978, a new law in New York State banned such opposition as discriminatory, allowing state or voluntary agencies to set up group homes in any residential neighborhood. But resistance still occurs in many places, and some group homes have been firebombed. During the late 1980s and early 1990s, this happened to six homes on Long Island, New York. Public attitudes and a lack of funding and staffing remain obstacles to providing adequate residential care for the mentally ill.

Improving access to treatment

It has been said that there are two systems of health care in America, one for the rich and one for the poor. People who can afford more care or have good insurance have access to private practitioners and hospitals. Those who lack such resources may turn to government-sponsored services. Inpatient care for the poor in public mental hospitals is still unpleasant in many places.

Yet insured people may also find themselves lacking the money to pay for mental health care. Insurance policies may reflect the attitude that mental health care is more self-indulgent and less necessary than physical care. Insurance companies also argue that some treatments are unproven. Coverage for mental illness is often less comprehensive, with more restrictions, than coverage for physical illnesses. Patients may be required to pay more of the cost of their mental health care, and there is less coverage for hospital stays, including limits on the total number of hospital days covered per lifetime. Policies range from covering a few visits to a psychiatrist a year to as many as fifty-two visits.

The difficulty of achieving reform

The experience of Mary Ann Beall and Raymond Bridge of Arlington, Virginia, shows the ordeal some people go through. Their daughter was diagnosed with paranoid schizophrenia and received costly treatments, both in hospitals and through private physicians. Within six years, they had used up the lifetime psychiatric benefits limits of five insurance plans and still owed more than $250,000. They were about to lose their home. Then new tests showed that their daughter had epilepsy, not schizophrenia. That meant that she had a new illness label for insurance purposes, a neurological disorder, not a mental one. As a result, she became eligible for full coverage.

When President Bill Clinton took office in 1993, he set health care reform as one his

President Bill Clinton's Task Force on Health Care Reform recommended expanded insurance coverage for many services related to mental illnesses, including drug rehabilitation and counseling for emotionally disturbed children.

priorities. Various reform plans were proposed and discussed as people debated what care should be covered. Tipper Gore, a psychologist and wife of Vice President Al Gore, was an outspoken advocate for achieving a balance between mental health care benefits and those for physical health care.

The health care plan that President Clinton proposed to Congress in 1993 provided mental health coverage beyond what many insurance policies then offered. Clinton said that mental health should not be viewed as less important than physical health. The President's Task Force on Health Care Reform recommended coverage for a broad range of services, including alcohol and drug abuse and more help for children with emotional disturbances. The task force had expressed concern about rising rates of mental illness, suicide, and mental hospitalizations among young people.

A 1994 poll conducted by the Judge David L. Bazelon Center for Mental Health Law showed that two-thirds of all Americans favored including mental health coverage in any basic national benefits package, and three-fourths thought this should be covered to the same extent as physical illnesses. Sixty percent said they would be willing to pay an extra $100 a year for such benefits.

Yet as the health care debate went on, various other bills were suggested, and some provided far less mental health coverage than the Clinton plan. As of 1995, Congress had not passed a health care reform package. A sluggish economy, budgetary limits, and a conservative political climate favoring less government contributed to this situation. Experts predicted that any successful reform package would have to limit benefits for mental disorders. Some proposed plans being reviewed by Congress did not cover alcohol or drug abuse, for example. Whether mental disorders will be treated like any others in future health care plans remains to be seen.

As has been true for years, underfunding prevents some people from receiving adequate treatment. Public programs usually serve the most severely sick and chronically ill. They often lack other resources, both social and economic. Only one in five poor children who needs mental health care receives it. Experts have called for more effective mental health legislation, along with funding for residential treatment programs and halfway houses and their staffs.

Reducing the stigma

Although the mentally ill are no longer viewed as witches or people possessed by demons, a stigma remains. In recent years, more people have come forward to share their experiences with mental illness and to reach out to others with

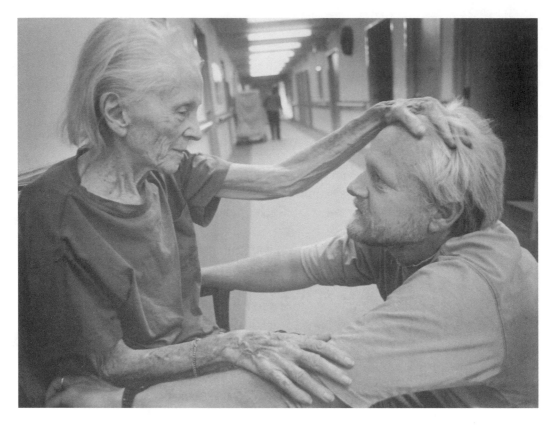

Mental disorders affect all sectors of society, causing pain and frustration for patients and their loved ones. In a private care facility, an Alzheimer's disease patient fails to recognize her son who has come for a visit.

problems. Well-known people have discussed their battles with drug and alcohol abuse, depression, suicide attempts, and eating disorders. People have described what it is like to live with mental illness or to see a family member suffer. Ordinary citizens also appear on television talk shows to air their problems, while mental health professionals add their insights to the discussion.

Mental health advocacy groups have worked to help the public realize that mental disorders are widespread and that they cause untold anguish to patients and their loved ones. Such exposure improves public awareness and encourages people to seek help. It can reduce the feelings of isolation that may engulf people with mental disorders. Education is still viewed as a key way to curb some mental and emotional problems, as

well as to reduce the prejudice and misunder-
standing that surround mental illness.

There is much optimism today about helping
the mentally ill. But this optimism is tempered by
some of the lessons of the past. According to Gerald Grob, history shows the importance of understanding that people with serious mental illnesses
may have quite different diagnoses, needs, and
outcomes. Says Grob, "There is no 'magic bullet'
that will cure all cases. . . . Like cardiovascular,
renal, and other chronic degenerative disorders,
serious mental disorders require both therapy and
management." Cures may not be found for every
disorder, says Grob, but we should keep trying to
help people live as best they can with their conditions. With more information, concerted efforts,
and adequate funding, there is hope of developing
the programs needed to relieve human suffering
and to help more people reach their full potential.

Glossary

acute: Of sudden onset and short duration.

affective: Relating to mood and emotions.

aftercare: Care provided to mental patients who have left institutions.

Alzheimer's disease: A condition characterized by degeneration of parts of the brain, resulting in loss of mental functioning, and, eventually, death.

anxiety: A feeling of dread, worry, or nervousness.

asylum: Institution for the mentally ill.

autism: Condition characterized by withdrawal from the outside world and inability to interact with others.

central nervous system: Consisting of the brain and spinal cord.

cerebral: Relating to the brain.

chronic: Of long-standing duration.

delusion: Belief that has no basis in outside reality.

dementia: Deterioration of mental abilities resulting in irrational behavior and emotional disturbances.

depression: Condition characterized by feelings of despair, sadness, and hopelessness.

group home: Supervised living arrangements for small groups of people.

halfway house: A supervised setting where former mental patients can live before returning to the community.

hallucination: Hearing, seeing, or sensing something that does not really exist.

hysterical paralysis: Paralysis brought on by mental, not physical, causes.

inpatient care: Care delivered to patients who are admitted to a facility for one or more nights.

involuntary commitment: Confinement against one's will for psychiatric care and treatment.

lobotomy: Surgical removal of part of the brain or the severing of major nerves in the front section of the brain.

mania: A state of agitated, frenzied behavior.

neurology: The study of the nervous system—brain, spinal cord, and nerves.

neurophysiologist: A scientist who studies the structure and functioning of the nervous system.

neurosis: A less severe mental illness often characterized by anxiety.

organic illness: Disorder stemming from biological or physiological causes.

outpatient care: Care delivered in a setting where people are not admitted to a facility overnight.

phobia: Unfounded fear that may prevent one from functioning in daily life.

psychiatrist: Physician (medical doctor) specializing in the care of people with mental illnesses.

psychologist: Professional with specialized training in the field of human behavior who may provide mental health services in the form of counseling, psychotherapy, or testing.

psychotherapy: Treatment of mental illness that focuses on its psychological—mental and emotional—aspects in order to change dysfunctional attitudes, feelings, and behaviors.

schizophrenia: Severe mental illness characterized by delusions, hallucinations, extreme withdrawal, and/or inappropriate mood.

Organizations
to Contact

Alcoholics Anonymous (AA)
475 Riverside Dr.
New York, NY 10163
(212) 870-3400

Alcoholics Anonymous is an organization for individuals recovering from alcoholism. AA maintains that members can solve their common problem and help others achieve sobriety through a 12-step program that includes sharing their experience, strength, and hope with each other. AA distributes several publications about its recovery program.

Alateen/Alanon
P.O. Box 862 Midtown Station
New York, NY 10018
(212) 302-7240
(800) 356-9996

Alateen and Alanon run programs for relatives and friends of individuals who have an alcohol problem. Alateen is specifically designed for young people age twelve to twenty whose lives have been adversely affected by someone else's drinking problem, usually a parent's. These organizations distribute a variety of informational newsletters and other publications.

Alzheimer's Association
70 East Lake St.
Chicago, IL 60601-5997
(312) 335-8700

The association provides information about this degenerative brain disease including resources for victims and families.

This organization also promotes research to find causes, treatments, and cures for Alzheimer's. It sponsors educational forums, operates a speakers bureau, and compiles statistics. The organization also publishes a newsletter.

National Alliance for the Mentally Ill (NAMI)

1901 North Fort Myer Dr., Suite 500
Arlington, VA 22209
(800) 950-NAMI

NAMI offers information about mental illnesses and treatments and sponsors self-help groups for patients and their families. The organization advocates increased research and services, including treatment, housing, and employment, as well as better insurance coverage for mental illnesses.

National Council on Alcoholism and Drug Dependence, Inc.

12 West 21 St., 7th Floor
New York, NY 10010
(212) 206-6770
(800) 622-2255

Through some 150 affiliates, this organization conducts prevention and education programs and helps people locate appropriate treatment programs in their region.

National Depressive and Manic Depressive Association

Merchandise Mart Box 3395
Chicago, IL 60654
(312) 642-0049

The association provides information about various depressive disorders and related conditions; some materials written about and for young people; lists of support groups in different areas.

Suggestions for Further Reading

Marie Balter, *Nobody's Child*. Reading, MA: Addison-Wesley, 1991.

Barbara Benziger, *Prison of My Mind*. New York: Walker, 1969.

Glenn Alan Cheney, *Drugs, Teens and Recovery*. Hillside, NJ: Enslow, 1993.

Davis Friedman, *Focus on Drugs and the Brain*. New York: Twenty-First Century, 1990.

Hannah Green, *I Never Promised You a Rose Garden*. New York: Signet, 1964.

Harvey Greenberg, *Emotional Illness in Your Family*. New York: Macmillan, 1989.

———, *Hanging In: What You Should Know About Psychotherapy*. New York: Scholastic, 1982.

Gerald N. Grob, *The Mad Among Us: A History of the Care of Mentally Ill Americans*. New York: Free Press, 1994.

———, *Mental Illness and American Society: 1875–1940*. Princeton, NJ: Princeton University Press, 1986.

Donna W. Guthrie, *Grandpa Doesn't Know It's Me: A Family Adjusts to Alzheimer's Disease*. New York: Human Science Press, 1986.

Robert Handly and Pauline Neff, *Anxiety and Panic Attacks*. New York: Rawson Association, 1985.

Margaret O. Hyde, *Mind Drugs*. New York: McGraw-Hill, 1981.

————, *The Homeless*. Hillside, NJ: Enslow, 1989.

Joel Kanter, *Coping Strategies for Relatives of the Mentally Ill*. Arlington, VA: Alliance for the Mentally Ill, 1984.

Bert Kaplan, *The Inner World of Mental Illness*. New York: Harper & Row, 1964.

Cynthia Copeland Lewis, *Teen Suicide: Too Young to Die*. Hillside, NJ: Enslow, 1994.

Marvin Lickey and Barbara Gordon, *Drugs for Mental Illness: A Revolution in Psychiatry*. New York: W. H. Freeman, 1983.

Robert A. Liston, *Patients or Prisoners? The Mentally Ill in America*. New York: Watts, 1967.

Mary McCracken, *A Circle of Children*. New York: Lippincott, 1973.

Don Nardo, *Anxiety and Phobias*. New York: Chelsea House, 1992.

Patricia A. O'Gorman and Philip Oliver-Diaz, *Breaking the Cycle of Addiction*. Pompano Beach, FL: Health Communications, 1987.

Neal H. Olshan, *Depression*. New York: Watts, 1982.

Elizabeth Schleichert, *The Life of Dorothea Dix*. New York: Twenty-First Century, 1991.

Susan Sheehan, *Is There No Place on Earth for Me?* New York: Random House, 1983.

Mark Vonnegut, *The Eden Express*. New York: Bantam, 1976.

Louise Wilson, *This Stranger, My Son*. New York: Putnam, 1968.

Works Consulted

Books

Silvano Arieti, *Understanding and Helping the Schizophrenic: A Guide for Family and Friends*. New York: Simon and Schuster, 1981.

Virginia Armat and Rael Jean Isaac, *Madness in the Streets: How Psychiatry and the Law Abandoned the Mentally Ill*. New York: The Free Press, 1990.

Gerald Caplan, *The Theory and Practice of Mental Health Consultation*. New York: Basic Books, 1970.

Ruth B. Caplan, *Psychiatry and the Community in Nineteenth-Century America*. New York: Basic Books, 1969.

Phyllis Chesler, *Women and Madness*. Garden City, NY: Doubleday, 1972.

Albert Deutsch, *The Mentally Ill in America: A History of Their Care and Treatment from Colonial Times*. New York: Columbia University Press, 1949.

Nancy Duin and Dr. Jenny Sutcliffe, eds., *A History of Medicine*. New York: Barnes and Noble, 1992.

Norman L. Farberow and Edwin F. Schneidman, *The Cry for Help*. New York: McGraw-Hill, 1961.

Robert H. Felix, *Mental Health: Progress and Prospects*. New York: Columbia University Press, 1967.

Michel Foucault, *Madness and Civilization: A History of Insanity in the Age of Reason*. New York: Random House, 1965.

Virginia Fraser and Susan M. Thornton, *Understanding "Senility."* Buffalo: Prometheus Books, 1987.

Sigmund Freud, *The Origin and Development of Psychoanalysis.* A series of lectures delivered in 1910. New York: Henry Regnery, 1965.

Institute of Medicine (U.S. Committee for the Study of Research on Child and Adolescent Mental Disorders), *Research on Children and Adolescents with Mental, Behavioral, and Developmental Disorders.* Washington, DC: National Academy Press, 1989.

Don D. Jackson, *Myths of Madness: New Facts for Old Fallacies.* New York: Macmillan, 1964.

Mary Ann Jimenez, *Changing Faces of Madness: Early American Attitudes and Treatment of the Insane.* Hanover, NH: Brandeis University Press, 1987.

Kathleen Jones, *Mental Health and Social Policy: 1845–1959.* New York: The Humanities Press, 1960.

Ari Kiev, ed., *Social Psychiatry.* New York: Science House, 1969.

Karl Menninger with Martin Mayman and Paul Pruyser, *The Vital Balance: The Life Process in Mental Health and Illness.* New York: Viking, 1963.

John C. Nemiah, M.D., *Foundations of Psychopathology.* New York: Oxford University Press, 1961.

Jim Orford, *The Social Psychology of Mental Disorder.* New York: Penguin Books, 1976.

Jonas Rappeport, *The Clinical Evaluation of the Dangerousness of the Mentally Ill.* Springfield, IL: Charles Thomas, 1968.

George Rosen, *Madness in Society: Chapters in the Historical Sociology of Mental Illness.* Chicago: University of Chicago Press, 1968.

Charles E. Rosenberg, *The Care of Strangers: The Rise of America's Hospital System.* New York: Basic Books, 1987.

Andrew Salter, *The Case Against Psychoanalysis.* New York: The Citadel Press, 1963.

Leonard A. Scheele, *The Orientation of Public Health.* Public Health Service Publication 436. Washington, DC: Government Printing Office, 1955.

Richard H. Sieden, *Suicide Among Youth.* Prepared for the Joint Commission on Mental Health of Children. Washington, DC: Government Printing Office, 1970.

George S. Stevenson, *Mental Health Planning for Social Action.* New York: McGraw-Hill, 1956.

Thomas Szasz, M.D., *Law, Liberty, and Psychiatry: An Inquiry into the Social Uses of Mental Health Practices.* New York: Macmillan, 1963.

———, *The Manufacture of Madness.* New York: Harper & Row, 1970.

———, *The Myth of Mental Illness.* New York: Harper & Row, 1974.

Michael Winerip, *9 Highland Road.* New York: Pantheon, 1994.

Shomer S. Zwelling, *Quest for a Cure: The Public Hospital in Williamsburg, Virginia, 1773–1885.* Williamsburg, VA: The Colonial Williamsburg Foundation, 1985.

Periodicals

Gabriel Constans, "This Is Madness: Our Failure to Provide Adequate Care for the Mentally Ill," *USA Today Magazine*, November 1991.

Allan M. Dershowitz, "Preventive Detention and the Prediction of Dangerousness, Some Fictions About Predictions," *Journal of Legal Education*, vol. 23, 1969.

———, "Two Models of Commitment: The Medical and the Legal," *The Humanist*, July/August 1971.

Robert H. Felix, "Mental Disorders as a Public Health Problem," *American Journal of Psychiatry*, May 1949.

Ian Fisher, "Bill Compels Care for Mentally Ill," *New York Times*, July 1, 1994.

Lisa W. Foderaro, "Albany Plans House Calls to Monitor the Mentally Ill," *New York Times*, April 24, 1994.

———, "Helping Parents with Mental Illness," *New York Times*, May 18, 1994.

———, "Mental Hospitals for Unwilling Gain Support in New York State," *New York Times*, June 17, 1994.

Daniel Golden, "Building a Better Brain," *Life*, July 1994.

Daniel Goleman, "Mental Health Professionals Worry over Coming Change in Health Care," *New York Times*, May 10, 1993.

———, "More than 1 in 4 U.S. Adults Suffers a Mental Disorder Each Year," *New York Times*, March 17, 1993.

Erica E. Goode, "How Much Coverage for Mental Illness?" *U.S. News & World Report*, March 14, 1994.

Melissa Grove, as told to L. Warner, " 'Now I Know I Want to Live,' " *Woman's World*, July 5, 1994.

Bob Herbert, "Sick and Cheated," *New York Times*, September 1, 1993.

Margot Hornblower, "Down and Out—but Determined: Does a Mentally Disturbed Woman Have the Right to Be Homeless?" *Time*, November 23, 1987.

Lisa Horton, "What Psychiatric Drugs Did to Me," *Glamour,* April 1993.

Charisse Jones, "Mentally Ill Homeless Man Goes to Bridgeport," *New York Times*, August 25, 1993.

Lewis L. Judd, M.D., "What Must Be Done to Ensure the Nation's Mental Health," *USA Today*, November 1990.

Jeanie Kasindorf, "The Real Story of Billie Boggs," *New York*, May 2, 1988.

Charles Krauthammer, "How to Save the Homeless Mentally Ill," *The New Republic*, February 8, 1988.

Albert Q. Maisel, "Bedlam 1946," *Life*, May 6, 1946.

Robert D. McFadden, "Homeless Man of West Side Is Held

Again," *New York Times*, September 26, 1993.

Michael J. O'Sullivan, "Criminalizing the Mentally Ill," *America*, January 11, 1992.

Daniel Pendick, "Chaos of the Mind," *Science News*, February 27, 1993.

Joan Philips, "The Crazy Lady: A Troubled Tenant Torments Her Co-Op Building," *New York*, April 2, 1990.

Elisabeth Rosenthal, "Who Will Turn Violent? Hospitals Have to Guess," *New York Times*, April 7, 1993.

R. Slovenko, "The Psychiatric Patient, Liberty, and the Law," *American Journal of Psychiatry*, vol. 121, December 1964.

Sidney Solloway, "Mental Illness—a Chemical Leprosy," *Westport (CT) News*, January 6, 1995.

Michael Stone, "Dance of Death: A Fatal Stabbing on West 69th Street Brings the Curtain Down on Two Lives," *New York*, August 19, 1991.

E. Fuller Torrey, M.D., "Homelessness and Mental Illness," *USA Today*, March 1988.

———, "The Mental Health Mess," *National Review*, December 28, 1992.

Anastasia Toufexis, "From Asylum to Anarchy," *Time*, October 22, 1990.

———, "Struggling for Sanity," *Time*, October 8, 1990.

Index

About the Author

Victoria Sherrow holds B.S. and M.S. degrees from Ohio State University. Among her writing credits are numerous stories and articles, six books of fiction, and more than forty works of nonfiction for children and young adults. Her recent books have explored such topics as public education in America, the role of the media in U.S. elections, and the U.S. health care system. Sherrow lives in Connecticut with her husband, Peter Karoczkai, and their three children.

Picture Credits

Cover photo: The Bettmann Archive
AP/Wide World Photos, 65, 89
Archive Photos, 44, 45, 52, 61, 85, 86, 88, 92, 98, 106
The Bettmann Archive, 24, 26, 29, 33, 47, 58
Colonial Williamsburg Foundation, 28, 35, 36
K. Condyles/Impact Visuals, 80
Dictionary of American Portraits, published by Dover
 Publications, Inc., in 1967, 34
Louis Fernandez/Black Star, 73, 74
R. Hitchman/Unicorn Stock Photos, 6
Evan Johnson/Impact Visuals, 11, 14, 100, 103, 108
John Launois/Black Star, 70
Library of Congress, 18, 43, 67
Christopher Morris/Black Star, 76, 77
National Library of Medicine, 16, 23, 25, 27, 32, 56
Courtesy New York Academy of Medicine; reproduced from
 the *Dictionary of American Portraits*, published by Dover
 Publications, Inc., in 1967, 63
North Wind Picture Archives, 22
Pamela Parlapiano/Impact Visuals, 54
Rick Reinhard/Impact Visuals, 9
C. Schmeiser/Unicorn Stock Photos, 96
UPI/Bettmann, 15, 38, 46, 49, 50, 59, 60, 91, 99